Cooking with Dad

by
R. J. Turner
and
T. J. Turner

© R. J. Turner & T. J. Turner, 1997

Turner Enterprises, L.L.C.
P.O. Box 2752, Winchester, VA 22604

Copyright 1997 by R. J. Turner and T. J. Turner

First Edition Published 1997

All Rights Reserved.

This book may not be reproduced in whole or in part, in any form without written permission from the authors.

Edited by R. J. Turner

Illustrations by
> Glenn Maurer, Glenn Maurer Graphics and T. J. Turner

Photos by R. J. Turner

Desktop publishing by Theresa Kilmer

Printed by Winchester Printers, Inc.

Published by Brian Smith

Printed in the United States of America

ISBN 0-9660920-0-7

To Mary, Wife and Mother

Acknowledgments

We want to thank all the women in our lives that have instilled our desire to have fun, learn, and eat.

Mary Mitchell Turner - Wife, mother, and better cook. She let us use her kitchen, as long as we did the dishes and reset the circuit breakers when we blew them. She also did some of the shopping. She has hundreds of cook books, which we never touched. She said, "I have never seen a cook book like this."

Elizabeth Mitchell - Mary's mother. A great cook in her own right. T. J. stays with her three to four weeks during the summer to fish and crab on the Chesapeake Bay.

Iva R. Turner - My mother. She is from the old school of meat, vegetable and potatoes: meat at 2 o'clock on the plate, vegetables at 7 o'clock, and potatoes at 11 o'clock - breakfast at 7:00 a.m., lunch at 12:00 noon and supper at 5:30 p.m. When I was a child, she would bake every Saturday morning. And — there was always dessert.

PREFACE

Cooking with Dad is a book written by me and my ten-year-old son. We had fun trying different combinations of food. We both learned from the experience.

Most of these recipes take one-half hour to prepare. This does not include the time to shop for the simple ingredients. This also does not include any time spent at the Emergency Room.

This book is filled with truths, half-truths and some down-right fibs. All are included to add to the adventure and enjoyment of cooking. Most of the fibs should be readily apparent, but they are so relevant I could not resist.

Cooking with Dad is a "how-to" and a "teaching" book. While making Pink Soup and "cleaning" a fish, you have an excellent opportunity to teach some history, physics, biology, chemistry, and math.

Have fun. Eat well. Learn lots. And don't let your child lick the paring knife.

P. S. T. J. and I welcome your recipes. If we use them in the next **Cooking,** you and your child(ren) will be listed in the Acknowledgments and I will send you a free copy of the new edition. This gives you Dads a great way to get your name in print without all the rigamarole we had to go through.

Please mail your recipes to the following.

>R. J. Turner and T. J. Turner
>**Cooking with Dad**
>Turner Enterprises, L.L.C.
>P.O. Box 2752
>Winchester, VA   22604

FOREWORD

For as long as I can remember, I have loved reading cookbooks. While I always enjoy new recipes, I read for the anecdotes about the origins of recipes, insights into regional specialties and, more recently, great advice on healthy eating.

Cooking with Dad is unlike any cookbook I have ever read. Most books have a recognizable beginning, middle and end; not **Cooking with Dad.** Most cookbooks assume that you know your way around the kitchen and already own (and use) your own cookware and utensils; not **Cooking with Dad**. Most cookbooks are concise, somewhat sophisticated and written for a serious cook; not **Cooking with Dad**. But, **Cooking with Dad** <u>is</u> something that most other cookbooks **<u>are not</u>**; it is **funny**.

Sheer desperation over the fact that I so often work late prompted my husband to theorize that : "If she can work ten hours, walk in the door and have dinner on the table in 30 minutes, what could be so hard about cooking?" And to conclude that : "If we can cook, we can eat sooner!"

At first, I felt a little guilty that my guys felt the need to write their own cookbook. After I read it, all guilt disappeared. It was clear they had learned where to find cookware and utensils in the kitchen (not a bad thing for the one charged with putting away clean dishes). They learned how to shop for their favorite ingredients. They gained a large measure of independence. And, clearly, they enjoyed themselves. I hope you do, too.

Mary Mitchell Turner

Table of Contents

INTRODUCTION

Cook's Tool Box 12
Survival Guide 20
What Do I Have?/What Can I Make? Matrix 25
Grocery Shopping 30

SECTION 1   BREAKFAST

PET - Potatoes, Eggs and Tomato 43
Dad's Egg Tower 48
Dad's Omelet 53

SECTION 2   LUNCH

Soups

Pink Soup 60
Turkey, Cheddar Soup with Peas 68
Noodle Soup with Meat 71
Yet Another Soup 73

Salads

Chunky Vegetable 76
Fruit Salad 82

Table of Contents (Cont.)

SECTION 3   DINNER

Stuffed Potatoes 93
Barbecued Fish 100
Barbecued Chicken 113
Cooking a Turkey 119
Tin Foil Supper 130

SECTION 4   DESSERT

Cakes
Chocolate Fish Cake 135

Cookies
Cookie Skyscrapers 149
Sort-of Rice Crispie Treats 153

Ice Cream Things
A Humdinger 157
Milk Shake 162

Pies
Coffee Spanish Cream 166

Table of Contents (Cont.)

SECTION 5   SNACKS

> Fruit Treats 172
> Grapefruit in "Blood" 174
> Bananas and Dates 175
> Peanut Butter and Jelly Bagel Pizza 177
> Math Munchies 179
> Tangy Fruit Drink 181
> Celery and Peanut Butter 183
> Meat Roll-Ups 185

Publications You Should Know About 188

Organizations You Should Know About 191

Cooking Measurements 193

Glossary of Terms 194

NOTES 196

Cook's Toolbox

Tool	Description
Band-Aids®	
Barbecue rack	
Briquettes	
Can opener	
Cutting board	
Dissecting kit	
Grater	with handle
Knife	table
Knife	paring
Masher	
Microwave	
Newspaper	
Pan	cookie or pizza
Paper towels	
Peeler	vegetable
Skillet	14", Wearever®
Sauce pan	with lid, 2 qt, Farberwear®
Spatula	long handle
Spoon	
Stove	
Tin Foil	
Whisk	

I like a Farberwear® two (2) quart sauce pan and lid as the basic implement in my cooking tool box. The pan heats up fast, which is good for children with a short attention span. Things do not stick to the bottom when being cooked if a minor emergency comes up while something is cooking — like getting a Band-Aid® or tourniquet. And most important, any amount of burnt-on food can be easily removed with hot water, a chisel, and scouring pad. The smooth, ergonomically designed handle also makes it easy to throw the pan and any "cooking failure" away.

    Frying Pan, 12 inch
    Pot, metal, at least 3.5 inches high, at least
        7 inches in diameter
    Measuring cup: two quart, clear, Pyrex®
    Ladle
    Spatula, long handle
    Spoon, long handle
    Grater with handle
    Peeler, vegetable
    Knives
        Chopping
        Fruit cutting
        Paring
        Table
    First aid
        Advil® (for the supervising cook)
        Aloe (for burns)
        Band-Aids®
    Grill

Stoves:

Gas is nice, but the flame attracts a child like a moth is attracted to a flame. Electric retains heat after it is turned off, so be careful you do not end up with a "branded" child.

Microwave Ovens:

Microwave ovens are one of the truly misunderstood kitchen appliances. They are not dangerous to human beings unless abused. How, you may well ask, can one abuse a microwave?

Microwaves cook using high frequency radio waves. (No, Johnny, you cannot hear the waves). The waves excite the center of the object in the microwave and start the water molecules vibrating. This vibration causes heat and the object cooks from the inside out.

Never put metal in the microwave. The energy waves do not like metal. You will see sparks and arcing — real cool, but if you allow this to occur you may see a reduction in your disposable income from buying a new microwave.

Likewise, do not use the microwave as a timer without having anything inside it. Running a microwave that is empty will ruin most microwaves.

Enough about what not to do. Let's show the kids some cool stuff.

Put a whole egg in the microwave. Put the setting on High for ten minutes and watch the egg explode. You, of course, will have to clean up the mess inside the microwave.

You can also explode a hot dog.

I was told you could also explode a potato, but that would be getting ahead of the recipes.

Beaters and Mixers:

There are many different kinds of beating or whipping implements. There is the manual labor whisk (don't ask me where it gets the name).

There are the kind that have two beaters where you crank a handle.

You can use the hand crank beater to teach your child about gears and ratios (the "nickname" for fractions).

On the cranking handle is a large gear. In the area where the beaters are held secure are smaller gears.

Use a ruler and measure the diameter of the large gear. (The diameter is a line that runs from one side of the gear to the other side and passes through the center of the gear, remember?)

Now measure the diameter of one of the small gears. This may be hard to do.

Estimates are OK.

Now divide the large number (gear) by the smaller number (gear). This number is called the gear ratio.

Example: (from my beater and T. J.'s measurements)

    Large gear   3-1/2 inches
    Small gear   1/2 inch

    Ratio   (7/2) / (1/2) = 7

The gear ratio means that, for every one turn (revolution) of the hand crank the small gear will go seven turns in the above example.

NOTE: The precise way to calculate the gear ratio is to count the number of teeth (ridges) on each gear. Then, use those numbers to calculate the gear ratio.

Now use the second hand on your wrist watch, second function of your digital watch, or a stop watch, if you have one.

Look at your watch.

Tell the child to crank the handle as fast as he or she can and count aloud each turn when you say "GO."

Say "GO."

When a minute is up, say "STOP."

You can now calculate the revolutions per minute (rpms) of the beaters.

Write down the number of turns of the crank handle your child did in a minute.

Multiply that number by the gear ratio.

The resulting number is the rpm of the beater.

You can have the children compete to see who is faster or you can have the child crank with the other hand.

Most children use their favored hand for most everything. By having them use the other hand, you will help in their overall development of coordination.

If the child has the same time with both hands then he or she may be ambidextrous — equally coordinated in both hands and both hemispheres of the brain.

If you have an old crank handle drill, you can put a beater in the chuck and let the child do it with the manual drill. Electric or hand drills are especially useful if you only have one beater, and it does not fit the one mixer you found. All the modern beaters have two for whatever reason, probably efficiency of time in blending and so forth.

For those of you who can't find the electric mixer or can only find the beaters; if you have an electric drill, hand-held of course (not one of those big ones that can go through concrete), your child might be interested in using that.

Electric hand drills are not quite as delicate and certainly don't go with the decor of the kitchen. But, they do work.

You can also teach the child some new words like "chuck." A chuck is the part you rotate to open the teeth so that the shank of the beater will fit. A chuck is adjustable. It will take a beater of any size.

Just like with a regular egg beater, you have to tell the child to keep the beater part, the blades, down into the solution before you turn it on and leave it down in the solution until you turn it off. Otherwise, especially with a drill going at maybe 1500 rpm's, it will fling the mixture all over the place. This is fun for the child. It can make interesting designs on the ceiling. But, is really difficult to clean up. Especially if you have high ceilings.

And then, of course, there is the unusual, messy way of whipping .... using a bull whip. Of course, this really doesn't whip the cream, but it is fun for the child to play with. You have to watch the child because he or she can lose an ear especially the right one if the child is right-handed or the left if the child is left-handed.

Survival Guide:

Clean Hands and Food:

Before you start cooking or preparing raw vegetables or food, you should wash your hands. You should then wash all fruit and vegetables. At the end of food preparation you should wash your hands again.

You should not keep putting your spoon or fork into a mixture to taste it to see if it is right and then putting it back in the mixture. You should use multiple spoons or wait until you think it is right and try tasting it once.

Certainly, if you drop the food on the floor you should pick it up and clean it off immediately (off the floor, that is) and throw away what landed on the floor.

Cleanliness is important to the health of every person who eats the food after you are done preparing or cooking. You may have something that really looks great, tastes great, but if you are uncomfortable with a stomach ache, diarrhea, or a headache for two or three hours after, that is no good.

NOTE: Most food poisoning events occur within one hour after eating.

According to researchers at the University of Arizona, Tucson, the biggest sources of kitchen germs are sponges and dishrags. One fifth of sponges and dishrags tested contained potentially deadly salmonella bacteria. Almost two-thirds had some bacteria that could cause sickness if ingested. Therefore, do not let your child eat sponges.

No. Seriously. Use germ-resistant sponges, and replace them frequently. Or, what I do is put a couple of squirts of Palmolive®-Ultra, concentrated antibacterial dish washing liquid on the sponge. I also use a lot of paper towels, which I throw away.

Always wash your hands before preparing food. This accomplishes two major things:

1) You won't spread germs.
2) You reduce your chances of getting sick.

You know what happens if your children get sick: a visit to the doctor, money for medicine, lost income from staying home with them, — plus, you will probably catch whatever they have.

Also, as a rule of thumb, empty the sink of all contents and put them away before starting to cook.

This teaches the child responsibility, and you both will know where things are stored. Now, your child knows that preparation is required for any project. Your significant other will appreciate the effort. And, it's about time the mess was cleaned up!

Have a big roll of paper towels handy for cleaning up spills and cleaning hands.

One last thing, nothing spoils a good experience or a good meal faster than a burnt tongue. So in the excitement and anticipation of eating a "concoction," make sure to have the child use a small spoon and blow on the first mouthful before putting the food in his or her mouth.

Basic Ingredients

The following is a minimum list of ingredients you should have to feed children.

Bread
Cereal
Dairy
    Cheese, sliced
    Eggs
    Milk
Fish
    Tuna
Fruit
    Apples - Red, Yellow and/or Green
    Bananas
    Blueberries
    Cantaloupe
    Cherries
    Dates
    Grapefruit, Red and/or White (No blue. Sorry.)
    Grapes
    Lemons
    Oranges
    Raisins
    Raspberries
    Strawberries
    Tangelos
    Tomatoes (Yes! They are a fruit, <u>not</u> a vegetable)

       Watermelon
Meat
       Chicken
       Hamburger
       Turkey
Spaghetti, No. 11
Soups
       Chicken Noodle
       Cream of Mushroom
       Cream of Tomato
       Vegetable Beef
Vegetables
       Broccoli
       Carrots
       Cauliflower
       Celery
       Corn, cream style and/or whole kernel
       Lettuce
       Peas, small
       Peppers, Green, Red and Yellow
       Potatoes, Red and/or White
       Tomatoes

What Do I Have?
What Can I Make? Matrix

Just in case you find yourself in charge of the food preparation ritual, you and your child may find the following matrix of value. I mean, how many children get a chance to use "Matrix Theory?"

What is a matrix? And, how will it stop me from being hungry?

A matrix is a pattern made with rows (left to right) and columns (up and down). Rows contain one type of information. This information, in the vocabulary of mathematics, is called independent. Independent events are things over which you have no control. When you open the refrigerator or cabinet, you have no control over what food-stuff is there. The columns, mathematically speaking, contain dependent events. Dependent events are things you have some control over, as a function of the independent events. The columns are the recipes you will find in this book. Where the rows and columns intersect is called a cell. The collection of cells give you what ingredients (row) you need to make the recipes (column).

Hey, and you thought long division was difficult?

Just read on, it will become easier to understand.

Steps to using the Matrix:

1) Go down the left column. Put "X"s next to the food stuff you have.
2) After you have completed that task, go across the row and circle each "X" in the table.
3) Find those columns that have all, or most of the "X"s circled.
4) Make a meal! (The number at the bottom of the table gives the page number for the recipes. The name at the top of the column gives the name of the meal, but who cares about the name. After all this work, you are only really interested in eating.)

WHAT DO I HAVE?/WHAT CAN I MAKE? MATRIX

Ingredient	BREAKFAST PET-Pizza	Pink Soup	LUNCH Another soup	Noodle soup
Bacon				
Bananas				
Beets, can of		X		
Bagels, Raisin-cinnamon				
Butter	X			
Carrots				
Cauliflower				
Cheddar				
Chicken, cooked		X		
Confectionery Sugar				
Cream-Style Corn				X
Cucumbers				
Dates, pitted				
Eggs	X			
Fish				
Grapefruit				
Hamburger				X
Jelly				
Maraschino Cherries				
Mashed Potatoes			X	
Meatloaf				X
Milk		X		
Mushroom Soup, can of		X		
Onions, Red				
Peanut Butter				
Peas, can of			X	
Peppers				
Potatoes, Red	X			
Rice, Minute®		X		
Salt & Pepper				
Sliced Cheese				
Spaghetti, cooked			X	X
Stoned Wheat Thins®				
Tomatoes	X			
Turkey				
Vegetable Beef Soup			X	X
Whole Kernel Corn			X	
Page Number	43-47	60-67	73	71-72

	DINNER			
Ingredient	Chunky Vegetable	Stuffed Potatoes	Turkey Cheddar	BBQ Fish
Bacon				X
Bananas				
Beets, can of				
Bagels, Raisin-cinnamon				
Butter				
Carrots	X			
Cauliflower	X			
Cheddar			X	
Chicken, cooked				
Confectionery Sugar				
Cream-Style Corn	X			
Cucumbers				
Dates, pitted				
Eggs				X
Fish				
Grapefruit				
Hamburger				
Jelly				
Maraschino Cherries				
Mashed Potatoes				
Meatloaf				
Milk				
Mushroom Soup, can of				X
Onions, Red				
Peanut Butter			X	
Peas, can of	X			
Peppers				
Potatoes, Red				
Rice, Minute®				
Salt & Pepper				
Sliced Cheese				
Spaghetti, cooked				
Stoned Wheat Thins®				
Tomatoes	X			
Turkey			X	
Vegetable Beef Soup			X	
Whole Kernel Corn				
Page Number	76-81	93-99	68-70	101-112

		SNACKS			
Ingredient		Grapefruit Halves	Bananas & Date	PBJ Pizza Bagel	Math Munchies
Bacon					
Bananas			X		
Beets, can of					
Bagels, Raisin-cinnamon				X	
Butter					
Carrots					
Cauliflower					
Cheddar					
Chicken, cooked					
Confectionery Sugar		X			
Cream-Style Corn					
Cucumbers					
Dates, pitted			X		
Eggs					
Fish					
Grapefruit		X			
Hamburger					
Jelly				X	
Maraschino Cherries		X			
Mashed Potatoes					
Meatloaf					
Milk					
Mushroom Soup					
Onions, Red					
Peanut Butter				X	
Peas, can of					
Peppers					
Potatoes, Red					
Rice, Minute®					
Salt & Pepper		X			
Sliced Cheese					X
Spaghetti, cooked					
Stoned Wheat Thins®					X
Tomatoes					
Turkey					
Vegetable Beef Soup					
Whole Kernel Corn					
Page Number		172	175	177	179

Grocery Shopping

First we are going grocery shopping. Few things are as exciting and anticipated with such enthusiasm as grocery shopping.

Just ask your child,

> Would you like to go to a movie?
> Would you like to go to the beach?
> Would you like to fly an airplane?

Well, you cannot do any of these things unless you are healthy. Being healthy is a function of what you eat. What you eat is directly related to what is in the refrigerator. And, the refrigerator is empty.

Therefore, we are going grocery shopping.

What is grocery shopping?

Grocery shopping (v) - 1) an obscene bodily function performed on a semi-regular basis, 2) a form of socialization for those over 25 years of age who have outgrown "the mall", 3) prehistoric characteristic programmed into our DNA that has to do with societal foraging.

Throughout this section I am writing about a store that may no longer exist in America. This is a store that is 20,000 to 30,000 square feet with parking for 100 to 200 cars. I am not talking about a "food warehouse" where you shop for your family or an Army battalion and you have fifty kagillion choices of 55-gallon drums, packages of 100, or a case of toilet paper for a year. I am also not talking about a gas station "convenience" store and deli where their motto is, "While you eat, let us fill you up with gas." These stores have one style of, say, corn; one supplier; and usually one (or none) can.

My mythical store has produce, that is crops produced from the land - maybe not American land, but somewhere on earth — like vegetables and fruit. It has things in various packaging: cans (tin and aluminum), boxes of card board, and "our friend" plastic bottles, so we can practice recycling. There is a dairy section, a meat section, and a fish section.

Clipping coupons from the Sunday paper is a good way to get the child involved in the shopping process. You can find out what the child likes to eat. You can also practice math by adding up the coupons you select to see how much money you will save. The child may want to split the savings with you by asking for half as a cash bonus.

TRADITIONAL GROCERY STORE LAYOUT

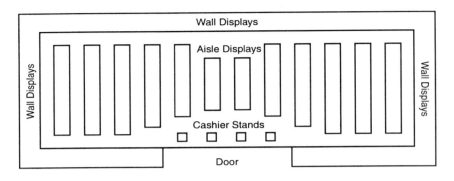

Figure 1

PATH THROUGH TRADITIONAL GROCERY

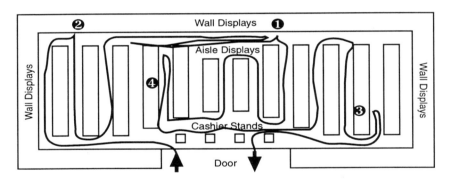

❶ Eggs
❷ Milk
❸ Bread
❹ Cereal

Figure 2

Why grocery shopping isn't so simple.

Personally, but what do I know, I feel that the whole grocery shopping experience could be simplified by having "food" in alphabetical order. Like ... bacon, beans, beef, broccoli ... No way!! Bacon needs to be refrigerated to preserve the nitrates (otherwise they may explode). Beans are in cans and need to be in the can section. Beef needs to be refrigerated. Broccoli is a "produce" and needs to be watered, even though it is definitely dead.

Organizing a grocery store alphabetically would put food beginning with "Z" at a disadvantage, as if zucchini needed help being discriminated against. Can you imagine the outcry and lobby efforts for alphabetically-disadvantaged vegetables?

Just put your list in a database program/application and sort alphabetically.

Figure 1 is a sample layout of a "typical" grocery store. Figure 1 is a top view. Figure 2 is the typical path to fill a "short" four (4) item list.

Aisles can be dangerous. Cartons of eggs can jump off the shelf and land on the floor. Glass containers will hurl themselves onto the floor to get attention. The produce section is earthquake prone: a symmetrical, pyramid structure of round produce cannot keep its shape if a lower element of the structure is removed! The other fruit in the pyramid, say, oranges, get mad if they're not picked and rush at the consumer, falling at his or her feet.

Shopping tips.

First, get a cart with wheels. **YOU CAN'T SHOP WITH THAT LITTLE BASKET THING.** As you spend time trying to find what you "need" on your list, you will soon find that your children find what they "need" from their favorite TV program. It is usually best to forbid the watching of TV for two (2) hours before going shopping — the memory time span of Smurf® and Barney® commercial promotional advertisements.

Personally, I find 5:30 a.m. the best time to shop. There are few people in the grocery store, my son is still groggy and the "I want ..." has not yet been booted-up to main memory.

Nevertheless, if your child(ren) is young, you **will** have to buy some of the things the child wants. Otherwise, the child may start to cry. Other shoppers naturally assume you abuse your child. Or, the child may become so irate he/she starts throwing things. This can be dangerous to other shoppers and may result in a personal liability suit. Whatever, another box of honey-coated cereal won't kill you or your child(ren).

Grocery shopping safety tips.

Cart Safety.

1) Do not leave a child unattended in the child carrying seat. The cart can tip over. Or, the child may be kidnapped.
2) Do not let the child hang on the cart. There have been legislative actions to have draw strings from sweat shirts removed. Children are being strangled when the strings get caught on something.
3) If you have more than one child, the bigger will want to push the smaller. That is usually a bad idea.
4) Do not let the child sit underneath the cart. They will put their hand or fingers on the floor as the cart moves. They can pick up pieces of glass and a wide variety of dirt and germs. Their fingers can be crushed by the wobbly wheels.
5) Do not let them hang on the front of the cart. The cart can become unstable and fall over.
6) The cart is not a "goal." No points are scored by pitching canned goods, frisbeeing frozen pizzas, or shot-putting chickens...into the cart.

You can let the child push if you are there to help. A child not tall enough to see over the cart, strong enough, or coordinated enough should not be allowed to push alone.

Do not let your children out of your sight. Give them whistles to wear when you are shopping. Tell them to just blow the whistle if they become disoriented or afraid.

How to impress the child(ren).

The produce section is the best section to impress your child. The highly refined techniques of how to select fresh fruits have been passed down from generation to generation starting with the Druids.

Bananas. Bananas are actually best if they have some small brown spots on them. (Small brown spots that move when you pick up the banana are called flies.) Usually the bananas are yellow with some green. These bananas are not really ripe and may take three or four days to reach softness and sweetness.

Cantaloupe. Hold the fruit between the palms of both hands. Push the end where it was attached to the stem with your thumbs. If the point is easily depressed, smell the fruit. If it is fragrant, the fruit is probably ripe.

Carrots. If the carrots are loose, the only proper way to test a carrot is with a carrot duel. Take the largest carrots and challenge the child to a duel. Actually you want small diameter carrots. If the

carrot is too large, there may be a hard, yellowish and pulpy center that you have to remove. Also, large diameter carrots are hard for a child to slice.

Celery. The stalk needs to be firm and stand tall. If it falls limp, it is old and has wilted.

Cereals. There are at least 397,455 different kinds of cereals. They all come in cardboard boxes. These boxes will not fit on your kitchen shelves. Once taken home, they rarely become empty. If you have one child let him/her pick a cereal in a small box.

Grapefruit. You have two kinds, white and pink. The pink is sweeter. The heavier the better.

Grapes. If there's anything white on the grape, like mold/fungus, the fruit is old and not even good to use in a sling shot. Also, avoid grapes with seeds. The child may swallow the seed and will never eat a grape again. Or, the seed will become a projectile used to hit the sibling. Generally, red grapes are sweeter than white grapes.

Lettuce. Since lettuce is sold by the head, the object is to find the heaviest head of lettuce — the most dense with the most leaves. (If you do not like lettuce, just do the opposite.) Take a head of lettuce in one hand and another head in the other hand. Find which one feels the heaviest. Now change hands to see if your sense of weight is biased to one side. (Right handed people usually have stronger right arms so something that feels heavy in the left, as opposed to the right, may actually weigh more.) Have the child try this and let him/her choose. Try five or six heads, putting back the lighter head each time.

Pastry. Gently squeeze your selection as you begin to pick it up to see if it is soft.

Soft = Fresh.

(A linear function with a direct relationship, as opposed to inverse relationship. Oh no, not more math?)

Unless you are going to pig out, one or two pastries per person is usually enough, more will only get stale.

Potatoes. There are two types of potatoes: red and white. The white potato is best for baking and making potato skins. The red potato is sweeter and has a softer skin. The sweetness seems to be preferred by children. Red potatoes are also the best for potato salads.

Oranges. Get NAVEL oranges. They are stamped "NAVEL." They have a little belly-button type thing on the top. These oranges have no seeds. Also, they are easy to peel.

Tangelos. A cross between tangerines and grapefruit. Look for ones without seeds. They are very sweet and very easy to peel.

Tomatoes. Tomatoes are actually fruit, not vegetable. Get this ... the fruit of the tomato is called meat. And to complicate matters even more, tomatoes can be red, yellow or green. Tomatoes can range in size from the biggest "Beef steak" tomatoes to the smallest "cherry" tomatoes.

Watermelons. Watermelons can be tested by thwopping the side in the middle. Thwopping is a physical act: place the nail of the middle finger against the thumb on the same hand, then thrust the finger forward at the watermelon. (Congratulations. You have just used a class-three lever.) This method should **not** be used by one child to check the ripeness of another child's head.

Do not try to do comparative shopping for the best price. All this unit pricing stuff will only frustrate you. On the other hand, if you want your child to learn math using a hand-held calculator, this is a great "real-life" opportunity to work math problems together. (Yea. Right!)

I suggest going for national name brands.

Section 1 - BREAKFASTS

Breakfast

Potatoes, Eggs and Tomato (PET) a Breakfast Pizza

You have probably heard of a B.L.T. - **B**acon, **L**ettuce, and **T**omato sandwich. This is a P.E.T. - **P**otato, **E**ggs and **T**omato breakfast pizza.

Food Fact or Fable?

Pizza was not invented in Italy. It was invented in Roswell, NM, during ... one of the many alien visits to earth. The symbols P-I-Z-Z-A look like the symbols we know as part of our alphabet, but actually the symbols are encriptions meaning "Earth people will eat anything that looks like pasture paddies". The pepperoni represent the numerous eyes of the aliens who brought the first pizza to earth in a spaceship that resembled a cow.

NOTE: Believe-it-or-not the Congress of the United States, in their infinite wisdom, has proclaimed "National Pizza Day". June 4 is the day chosen for this important national holiday.

Pizza History: Cato, a Roman statesman and author, got the "ball rolling" in approximately 200 B.C.

(Before Crust). He wrote about flat rounds of baked dough topped with olive oil and herbs.

Pizza historians think pizza arrived in the U.S. when Italians began immigrating here in the 1890's. From this humble beginning Americans have taken the basic sauce-and-cheese format and Americanized it. Toppings now range from the traditional sausage, pepperoni, green peppers to anchovies, pineapples and just about anything else people can stomach.

Ingredients:

3	Potatoes, small red (or 1 big potato)
4	Eggs
1	Tomato
1 tsp.	Butter

Tools:

Frying pan
Knives
Cutting board
Spatula
Stove
Microwave (optional)

This recipe could also be called an "egg helper," since it makes it look like you have more eggs than you do.

Get two or three small (or one large) red potatoes and one tomato. Put the egg carton on the counter. Next take out 3 eggs and put them near the potatoes. The amount of eggs (by volume) should equal the amount of potatoes. Just eyeball this.

Wash the potatoes and tomato under cold water with dish soap. Use some kind of scrubber for the potatoes to get off the dirt.

Do not peel the potatoes. Many vitamins and nutrients are in the layers of skin.

Thinly slice the potatoes and tomato and slice them in thin slices. You can then let your child cut the slices into small pieces.

While the child is chopping the potatoes and tomato, melt about one teaspoon (the smaller spoon) of butter in a frying pan by setting the unit one-half way to high.

Take the chopped up potatoes and put them in the frying pan. The butter will brown the potatoes and add flavor. Make sure the potatoes do not stick and burn because burnt is not the flavor we want. Let the child stir and flip the potatoes with a spatula. You can turn the temperature control to 2/3 of the way to high.

Check to see if the potatoes are getting soft. (Nothing will stop a child from eating faster than finding something hard in scrambled eggs.) The child is prepared for the soft consistency of scrambled eggs, not the hard crunchiness of raw potatoes.

If you have a lot of potatoes (four-egg quantity or more), I suggest the following to speed up the "softening" process.

After the potatoes have become brownish, get a plate. Put a piece of paper toweling on the plate. Pour the potatoes from the frying pan onto the paper toweling, and turn the unit off. Pull up the corners of the paper toweling to make a pouch and then turn it over on the plate. Place the plate in the microwave and nuke them for two to three minutes. This will make the potatoes soft faster.

Now pour the potatoes back into the frying pan and turn the unit back on to 2/3 of high. Put in the chopped up tomato. Finally add the eggs.

You may want to teach your child how to crack the eggs with a table knife, but I suggest you put the eggs in to minimize the amount of egg shells in the mixture. Why go through all the trouble of softening the potatoes and then put in egg shells???

Let the child stir and flip the contents of the frying pan until it is all mixed up. Cook until the eggs are firm.

If you want, you can form the mixture into a circle in the frying pan just before you serve it. Then cut the PET into slices. Serve as a "breakfast pizza."

Dad's Egg Tower

Looking for a high protein, hot, easy-to-make-breakfast? And something to build? with your child? Dad's Egg Tower is a good one because your child can be involved during most of the preparation and cooking.

Ingredients per serving:
- 2 Eggs
- 1 Bread, slice
- 1 Cheese, slice
- 1 Meat, slice (ham, turkey, pepperoni, etc.)
- Butter
- Salt and pepper or Mrs. Dash® seasoning

Tools:

- Frying pan
- Knife
- Spatula
- Toaster
- Stove

Place the frying pan on one of the stove's large heating elements. Turn the heat control for that unit one-half way to hot (medium).

Place a teaspoon full of butter in the frying pan. The butter will grease the pan so that the eggs will not stick. Even if you have one of those "no-stick pans," I would still use butter, just in case, plus the butter will add flavoring to the eggs.

Use the spatula to spread the melted butter around the surface of the frying pan. Have the child spell out their initial, or C-A-T, or better yet, E-G-G.

Take two eggs. We like Grade A, medium eggs. Put one egg in the palm of one hand. With the table knife in the other hand, hit the egg in the middle with the blade side with a blow sufficient to crack the shell, but not Rambo enough to go completely through the egg. You want to break the shell enough so that you can easily separate the shell into two pieces and pour the egg's contents into the frying pan. If you decide to pull a Rambo, you will find that little pieces of the shell will be distributed in the albumen (the clear part that cooks up white) and the yolk (the yellow part). Crunchy, shell-laced eggs are not acceptable to most children.

Depending on the age and the hand-eye coordination of your child, he or she can crack the eggs. If you have a young child, you hold the egg and let the child crack the egg with the knife.

Once the egg is cracked, empty the contents into the frying pan.

If you want the child to put the eggs into the frying pan first take the hot pan to the table. Put a hot pad or pot holder under the frying pan. You should be ever vigilant that no pieces of the egg shell fall into the hot pan. The child might try to remove the shell with his/her fingers, which may cause a burn or scald from the hot butter. You may want to break the yolk with a knife so that it will mix with the white part. The child can do this. Put the pan back on the stove heating unit

Now put the bread into the toaster. Most toasters have a temperature control in the front. This is usually a little black lever that can be moved from side to side. The far left side will produce toast that looks like bread, the far right setting will produce toast that looks like charcoal. I suggest the middle.

If you are using more than one type of bread for different children, you will most definitely need to experiment. Or, just leave the lever in the middle and get the egg onto the toast fast enough to cover it before the comments fly.

The degree of "toastiness" has to do with the extent to which the sugar in the bread is oxidized. With multi-grain breads, the various grains will be toasted to varying extent to add another degree of darkness, texture and a dimension of taste.

We like Home Pride®, ButterTop®. It is a multi-grain, sort of sweet, brown bread.

Back to the frying pan.

> **CAUTION:** If your child is standing on a chair by the stove, make sure you have an arm around your child's waist. If the child bends down or leans over the frying pan to break the yolk he/she may lose his/her balance. The child may use hands to break the fall with the hand(s) going into the hot frying pan or hitting the handle, thereby launching the eggs and hot butter. The hot butter could land on the child's face.

Put a slice of meat in the frying pan beside the eggs and heat it thoroughly. If you put the meat on the toast directly from the refrigerator, it will cool the toast and eggs too fast.

When the eggs start to have bubbles, it is time to separate them from each other and flip them. Use the spatula. Clean the edge of the spatula before attempting to flip the eggs. If the edge is not clean, the eggs cannot be effectively flipped. You can have the child hold the spatula and you hold his or her hand and help with the flipping.

After the flip, turn the stove unit off.

Leave the eggs in the pan.

A slice of cheese can now be put on one of the two eggs by the child. Even with the unit off, with an electric stove there will be sufficient heat in the unit and in the egg to melt the cheese.

The toast should be done by now (if the toaster is plugged in).

Put the toast on a plate.

Spread some butter on the toast.

Put the meat on the toast.

Put the egg with the cheese on top of the meat

Remember the cheese will be hot.

Put the other egg on top.

Eat with a knife and fork.

Have the child blow on small pieces so that he/she will not burn his/her mouth.

Don't forget the orange juice!

Dad's Omelet

Ingredients:

2 per person	Eggs
1 slice per person	Cheese
1 tbsp per person	Cottage Cheese
Some	Meat - ham, chicken, bacon hamburger, or sausage
	Salt and pepper

Tools:

Frying pan
Knife
Whisk
Bowl, deep
Ladle
Spoon

If the meat is pre-cooked all you have to do is heat the meat while you are cooking the egg mixture.

If the meat is uncooked, cook the meat first. Remember pork needs to be cooked until very well done in order to eliminate the possibility of contracting trichinosis.

Trichinosis is a disease that you can get from eating under cooked pork infected with Tridinellal Spiralis parasites. The disease in humans is first characterized by diarrhea, nausea, fever and then you get really sick. The disease in humans is caused by small worms in the intestines and tissues and causes pain whenever the muscle is used.

Remember, **NEVER EAT RARE PORK**.

Break the eggs into a mixing bowl.

You can hold the egg while the child hits the egg with the blade edge of a table knife. You can empty the contents of the egg shell into the bowl or you can have the child separate the egg shell by placing both thumbs in the crack and pulling the two pieces of the shell apart.

If you let the child separate the shell, check to make sure none of the egg shell goes into the bowl.

No one likes crunchy eggs!

For every two eggs per person put a tablespoon (Yes, the large spoon) of cottage cheese into the bowl.

I like small curd cottage cheese. It mixes better with the egg and makes a fluffier omelet.

Use the whisk to mix the eggs and cottage cheese.

The child can do this if the bowl is deep, say six (6) inches, and the child does not mix too strenuously.

Put the frying pan on the stove. Turn the dial of the unit 2/3 from ON. Put in a pat or small amount of butter.

Now pour the mixture into the frying pan or have the child use a ladle. Fill the frying pan until about half the pan is covered.

You can use the edge of the spatula to stop the egg mixture from flowing as the heat makes the egg firm.

We put the meat into the other half of the pan to heat it.

When the egg starts to bubble, use the spatula to divide the egg in half.

Flip each half over and turn off the heat.

Put cheese, sliced or grated, on one portion of the egg.

Then put the meat on the cheese.

Now put the other half of the egg on top.

The heat from the frying pan and from the eggs will melt the cheese and wrap around the meat.

Take the omelet (which is really not an "official" omelet) and put it on a plate to serve.

Section 2 - Lunch

Soups

Pink Soup

Ingredients:

1 can	Mushroom soup
1 can	Beets, cooked
	Beet juice, save enough to make the soup pink
1 soup can	Milk
1 soup can	Minute Rice®
1 soup can	Water
	Chicken, broiled (in this case the night before)

Tools:

Saucepan
Whisk
Spoon
Can opener
Stove

Time: One-half Hour (or longer if you have to go to the Emergency Room).

Open the can of mushroom soup. This may need supervision depending on the age and curiosity of the child. Smaller children may not be able to use the can opener to do the initial puncturing of the can top, but may be able to turn the handle to cut the top from the can.

Opening cans can be dangerous because the can's rim and the lid are both extremely sharp — dangerous. Take a pot holder, grasp the lid and carefully take the lid off (or out of the soup). You can then demonstrate the danger from the sharp edge by using the lid to slice a potato. Then let your child hold the pot holder and lid and let the child cut a potato. (Better now with you watching, than later when you are not looking.)

Why cut a potato, you may ask?? Well, humans have skin and potatoes have skin. It is better to cut the "skin" of a potato as a demonstration, than to have your child cut his/her skin by mistake.

As the Chinese (did not say), "A good demonstration is worth a thousand Band-Aids®."

Put the lid in a safe place for disposal later.

Keep the can. You will use it for measuring later.

Mushroom soup does not pour. Therefore, when your child is trying to pour it, say "Here is a spoon to help you". Already you show how smart you are in the kitchen. Yea, Dad!

After you have spooned the soup into the saucepan, use the can to measure the milk. Have the child pour the milk into the can. The pouring should be performed in or near the sink. This feat shows the effect of gravity; i.e. things fall to earth, but not necessarily where you think they will. A three-year-old may not be able to handle a one gallon bottle alone. Four-year-olds and up are experimental or adventurous with all liquids, pouring from great heights is always exciting, if not wasteful. Having the can in or near the sink makes it easier to clean up the inevitable spill(s).

Pour the milk into the saucepan with the soup. Use a spoon or whisk to have the child mix the soup globs with the milk. This can be done on the counter, a table or on the stove. I do not recommend on the stove. If the mixture slops out onto the heating element, the heated mixture will smell bad and may also create smoke. Both events may be exciting for the child, but may reduce the probability the child will eat the finished product.

A gas stove can be dangerous. The stirring process usually causes the pan to move away from the child, toward the back of the stove. As the child reaches to continue the stirring process, the clothing may come in contact with the open flames. This is not recommended.

Turn the stove on to medium or equivalent. At this temperature the milk should not burn while the rest of the stuff is being prepared, even if someone forgets to occasionally stir the mixture.

BE CAREFUL, WATCH THE CHILD

Make sure you have a spoon with a handle longer than the diameter of the pan. If the spoon has a short handle, I bet you a dollar the spoon will end up in the bottom of the pan. (Send the dollar to T. J. Turner's College Fund, P.O. Box 2752, Winchester, VA 22604.) Then, the child will reach into the mixture to get the spoon. This may result in scalding the child if the soup is hot. Or, at a minimum, a messy hand(s) which may be made clean by vigorously shaking. Try cleaning mushroom soup from the ceiling or explaining what is on the ceiling to your significant other!

It just so happens, we have some chicken left over from a couple of nights ago. Pull the meat from the bones. Throw away the skin. Use a chopping board and knife to cut the chicken into small pieces.

> Even previously crispy skin or coating becomes soggy in a soup. Do not put the skin in the soup or you may hear what T. J. said: "Dad, why did you put lettuce in the soup?"

Try not to have any pets in the kitchen. Our Irish Setter can smell cold chicken five miles away. A begging animal takes the child's attention away from the project. Petting the animal results in "furry hands"— chicken grease is one of the best adhesive materials known to mankind — What do you think is on the back of Post-Its®?? (I don't know either.)

Pour the sliced, diced, and chopped chicken into the saucepan and stir. Have the child stir in one direction ten times and then stir ten times in the other direction. This helps teach counting, hand-eye coordination, makes him/her ambidextrous, and makes you look like a karate expert. ("The Karate Kid," wax-on-wax-off).

Open the can of beets. Use the same precautions as with opening the can of mushroom soup.

Let the child pour a small amount of beet juice into the soup. The soup will immediately become pink. Yes, this is like the pink snow in <u>Return of the Cat in the Hat</u>. This is an example of dispersion, where a small amount of one substance affects a larger substance. A cook and a teacher. Good going, Dad.

Pour the rest of the beet juice down the sink drain.

Pre-cooked beets are easy to cut for any age child with only a table knife. You may want to cut the beets in half and put the flat side on the cutting board. This reduces the probability of having a beet fly across the room or onto the floor. Beets on the floor have a 101% probability of being stepped on.

Beets on the floor are from the banana peel family — need I say more?

You can leave a little pool of beet juice on the counter. Get the largest bandage you have and put on the child's hand. When the significant other comes in, it will be assumed that a near tragedy has happened. The cook must have a good handle on the relationship with the S.O.G. (**S**ignificant **O**ther **G**irl/**G**uy) and the potential outcome of such a prank.

Pour the diced beets into the saucepan.

Use the soup can again to measure one-half a can of water. Use a spoon to get any soup and milk still clinging to the can. Pour into the saucepan.

Now pour in one-half a soup can filled with Minute Rice®.

Stir the soup in the saucepan until it starts to boil. More physics. The heat from the cooking unit is passed to the metal saucepan through conduction (if an electric stove) or through radiation (if a gas stove). The heated metal passes the heat through conduction to the mixture. Bubbles appear on the surface, when the soup boils. The mixture is now at 212°F or 100°C. The water on the surface of the soup is now evaporating, turning from a liquid to a gas.

Do not let the child stick his/her face into the pot to "smell the soup." The bubbling surface may cause the steam from the scalding liquid to burn his/her face.

Pour in the rice. Stir the rice to make sure it is not just floating on the surface. Put the lid on the saucepan. The evaporating water vapor causes the rice to fluff up and become soft. If you do not have a top that fits, put a frying pan or plate on top of the saucepan. You need some kind of cover so the rice will fluff up.

Turn off the stove.

Remove the pan from the unit. If you leave it on the unit of an electric stove, the unit stays hot and will continue to cook the soup. This may burn the milk and stuff on the bottom. This causes smells and tastes that may be rejected by the child. "Oh, yuck! I'm not going to eat this stuff."

Stir the mixture in about five minutes. The Minute Rice® will fluff up in about ten minutes: nothing is worse than serving uncooked rice for the following reasons.

"Dad, where did the bones come from?"
"I think I lost a tooth in the soup."
"I just broke my tooth."
"Yuck, I just ate a beet stem."

Female children will like the pink color better than males. The males will think it is interesting, but may not be motivated to eat it. Just tell them they can add chocolate syrup to it. **ONLY KIDDING, DAD**.

Turkey, Cheddar Soup with Peas

Ingredients:

1 ounce	Cheddar cheese
1 can	Peas
1 can	Beef-base soup (Vegetable Beef)
Some	Turkey
	Minute Rice®

Tools:

Can opener
Spoon
Grater
Saucepan and lid
Knife
Cutting board

Ask your child(ren) if they like the white or dark meat - children usually prefer the white meat.

Cut some slices of meat off the turkey.

Have the children cut the slices into strips. Then have them cut the strips into pieces.

Open the can of soup. **Remember the edge of the top is dangerously sharp**.

Pour the soup into the sauce pan. Fill the can with water. Add this to the saucepan.

Put in the cut up turkey.

Open a can of peas. Children like the small tender peas. I prefer the Le Sueur® brand of "Very Young Small Sweet Peas".

Pour in the peas and the liquid.

Turn the unit temperature to 1/2. You need to keep stirring the mixture so that it will not stick to the bottom of the pan.

After about five minutes, you can turn the temperature up to a 3/4 turn. Keep stirring. If any of the ingredients stick to the bottom of the pan, it may burn. Burnt matter does not smell or taste good — "Yuck, I don't like this Daddy."

Fill the soup can with Minute Rice®.

When the mixture starts to boil, pour in the rice. Remember to stir the rice into the liquid.

Take the pan off the unit, put the top on, and let it set.

Turn off the unit.

In about five minutes, stir the mixture in the saucepan.

Spoon the mixture into a bowl and grate cheese on the top. As the soup cools the cheese will melt into the soup.

Noodle Soup with Meat

Ingredients:

    1 can   Cream style corn
    1 can   Beef base soup
                       (vegetable beef)
    Some   Cooked spaghetti
    Some   Hamburger/meatloaf

Tools:

    Can opener
    Spoon
    Saucepan and lid
    Knife
    Cutting board

Take leftover spaghetti and cut it into short pieces. Just take a knife, even a table knife for a very young child, and have them cut a pile of spaghetti in different directions. Even the youngest child with the dullest knife can cut cooked spaghetti.

Open a can of soup. **Remember the top is dangerously sharp.** Pour the can of soup into the saucepan. Fill the soup can with water and pour the water into the saucepan.

Put the chopped-up spaghetti into the saucepan.

Open the can of cream style corn and pour the contents into the pan.

We had some leftover meatloaf. I took the "loaf" and cut it into slices. I then had T. J. cut the slices into pieces.

Put everything into the saucepan.

Turn the temperature up to 1/2 and start to stir, so that it will not burn to the bottom of the pan.

This soup is cooked and ready to serve as soon as all ingredients have been thoroughly heated.

Yet Another Soup

This is a true leftover soup.

Ingredients:

    1 can   Vegetable beef soup
    1 can   Peas
    1 Can   Corn
    Some   Mashed potatoes
    Some   Spaghetti, cooked

Tools:

    Can opener
    Sauce pan
    Spoon
    Stove

Open a can of vegetable beef soup. Pour the contents into the pan. Use the soup can to measure a full can of water. Add it to the saucepan.

We added peas, left over from last night's meal.

We also had about a half cup of mashed potatoes. Add that to the pan. Mashed potatoes go into solution and add texture.

T. J. and I were going to go trout fishing. In our section of northern Virginia, the trout like to bite on corn. We have no idea why. Trout cannot digest corn. Anyway, we had a part of a can of whole kernel corn that T. J. had gone through to get the largest kernels to fish with.

We put the rest of the corn and the corn juice into the pan.

We also have some spaghetti leftover from three nights ago. You or the child can cut the spaghetti into small pieces like the "noodles" in noodle soup.

Throw that into the pan.

Turn the unit on 2/3 of the way to high. Since there is now a lot of stuff in the pan, someone has to stir it so that nothing sticks to the bottom and burns.

When the soup starts to boil, it is too hot to eat, but it is fully cooked.

Turn off the stove. Spoon or ladle into bowls. Wait until cooler to eat.

Salads

Chunky Vegetable Salad

Ingredients:

1	Cucumber
1	Pepper
6	Carrots
1 head	Cauliflower
2	Tomatoes

Tools:

Pan
Knives
Peeler

All peeling should be done over the sink to aid in clean up.

Have the child peel a cucumber. Make sure the child peels away from himself/herself. Also make sure all fingers are behind the peeling area. Remember a peeler takes off the skin of the vegetable, but can also take the skin off of the "peeler."

The child may play a game — try to cover the largest area with the peelings. This game should be anticipated and discouraged.

Another game, if there is a window near the sink, is trying to have the peelings stick to the window. This game should also be discouraged.

When half the cucumber is peeled, turn it around to peel the other end. The peeled end is slippery. Make sure the child does not grasp it too firmly and launch it onto the kitchen floor.

Once the cucumber is peeled, you should cut it in half lengthwise. Start at the end furthest from you and draw the knife towards you. Make sure your fingers are not in line with the knife blade. Place the two halves with the flat side down so that the child can cut them into slices, lengthwise and then cut them into pieces.

If your child does not like the cucumber seeds, you should cut the halves of the cucumber in half again (i.e.; quarters). Then you can take a knife and cut the seed portion out of the quarter section. Then give the de-seeded cucumber back to the child to slice and chop up.

Put the cut up cucumber into a bowl. I like to put the veggies into a two quart Tupperware® container. Tupperware® has lids that seal so tight that this allows the chopped up pieces to be mixed by the child by shaking the container. (**Make sure the lid is on tight**.) Also, the lid stops odors from getting into the salad or out of the salad mixture, when in the refrigerator.

Take the pepper and wash it in cold, running water.

You should cut the pepper in half and cut out the seeds inside.

Give the child the halves to be cut in strips. The strips can then be held together in a bundle to be cut in smaller pieces.

Put the pepper pieces in the container.

Now we will do the cauliflower.

Cauliflower, in my opinion, is one of the least cost-effective vegetables. You throw away over one half of what you start with. But, it does look like a human brain, and what child could resist "performing brain surgery?"

The most difficult part about preparing cauliflower is getting it out of the plastic wrapping. Forget trying to untie the knot. Just take a knife and cut the plastic off.

Cut off all the green vegetation that comes with the "head" of cauliflower. This results in only the white portion.

Wash the white portion under cold running water.

Throw the plastic and green portion away. The green vegetation on the kitchen floor is part of the banana peel family.

Have the child cut off several of the globes. Make sure the stems are cut off so that only the outer part is left. Let the child cut up the sections into small pieces. These sections can also be pulled apart, but, of course, using knives is more exciting.

Use one half a head of cauliflower for every four people, unless you "really" like cauliflower. You should know that, cauliflower is one of the few vegetables that can produce gas. (No, cars will not be powered by cauliflower ... the other gas!)

Put this cauliflower into the mixture.

Now to the carrots.

Don't forget the child(ren) have been holding knives for the past 15 minutes. Have a short "sword fight" with the child(ren) using the longest carrots.

Take three or four carrots and peel them. Use the same method as the cucumber.

You should cut off the ends. Some of the ends have green vegetation on them. These can be put in a shallow bowl with water and over several days the child can watch a carrot grow. The carrot top will grow unless the following happens:

1) the water evaporates because "someone" forgets to add water,
2) the animals drink the water, or
3) "someone" does not know this is an experiment and throws it out.

I believe, but never have been able to prove, that carrots have a grain, just like wood. I find it easiest to cut the carrots length-wise placing the smaller end away from me and pulling the knife towards me. (Which is not really safe.) Then, take the halves and lay the flat sides down and cut length-wise again.

If the carrots are old, the center will be a different color than the outer layers. If this is the case, you may want to cut out the inner section like you cut the seed portion of the cucumber out of these quarter sections.

Now the child can cut the carrot spears into small pieces.

Put the pieces into the mixture.

Wash the tomatoes. You should cut them into slices and have the child cut the slices into pieces.

Celery is another clumpy vegetable. Cut off about one inch of the bottom part. Pull each of the stalks of celery off the heart and wash separately. Cut off the greenery on the top, if any, just below the thing that looks like a ring. If the celery is limp, put the individual stalks into a bowl. Add water and put in the refrigerator for several hours. The celery will take in the water and become stiffer. This is due to the capillary action of the cells in celery.

Children sometimes do not like celery because it is "stringy". This "string" runs the length of the celery stalk. The outer stalks are stringier than the inner stalks. For this reason you may not want to add the outermost stalks. You can also pull off some of the strings by using the peeler to take off the outer layer of the outer stalks.

Celery is easy to cut up. Just draw the knife down the center of each stalk. Then cut the strips into pieces.

Put the celery in the mixture.

Mix the mixture or shake the Tupperware® - **with the top on firmly.**

The salad is done.

Fruit Salad

My wife and I believe that the words "no" and "don't" are used far too much by parents. "Yes" is a more positive word, gives a more positive outlook on life. When you go down the list of possible ingredients for this recipe, ask your child to say yes to those ingredients he or she wants or remain silent.

Ingredients:

2	apples; red, yellow and/or green
1	banana
1	cantaloupe
20	cherries
some	dates
2	grapefruit
4	oranges
2	peaches
1/2	pineapple
some	raisins
some	red grapes
some	white grapes

Tools:

    Apple corer
    Cherry pitter
    Colander
    Knives
    Strainer

You really don't need all the above, but if you include them all you will get all kinds of vitamins, minerals, textures, and tastes. And, most important to T. J., he gets to use different kinds of tools. Your child could have a lot of input into what and how much goes into this recipe.

Make sure you get rid of the seeds first, because almost no one likes seeds. Fruit salads are sometimes not chewed, they are sort of squished between the tongue and the top of the mouth and swallowed. A large seed will detract from the excitement of doing that by getting stuck in or scratching the throat.

> **Note:** It doesn't matter if a child swallows a seed. The seed will pass through eventually in two to three days. But, the sensation may have a negative impact on their interest in eating fruit.

Let me point out that all of these seeds that you are going to be throwing away could be kept, dried, and planted with an approximately 70% probability of growing a plant. Now, for those of you in the inner city, you may not want to have a grapefruit or cherry tree, but it might be interesting to try. The experiment will teach the child a little about plant physiology and botany.

Wash the seeds. Lay them on a plate. Put the plate in the direct sunlight or underneath a light bulb that has a shade that will direct the heat downward. This will dry the seeds.

Once they are dried, say in 24 hours, take them and put them in a small bowl of water. Don't mix the seeds up or you won't know which seed is from which fruit.

The seeds should split apart and you will see a little green growth in a few days. You have to remember to keep water in the dish. (T. J.'s cats like to drink seed-sweetened water.) This is the beginning of a root. Now, you need to put the "germinating" seeds in potting soil, which you can get from a hardware store.

Grapefruit and Oranges:

Take the grapefruit and put your left index finger on the top where it was disconnected from the tree. Rotate it 90 degrees, or one quarter turn, to your left. Have the child cut through the middle. As it opens, you will see little sections.

With a paring knife or a knife with a short blade, you can cut out each section.

When you cut up the grapefruit and oranges have the child squeeze the rind, that's the outer part, to get the juice out. If a child can't squeeze it with one hand have them put the rind between the palms of both hands. Lock their fingers together. Push their palms together. Once you push one direction rotate the rind 90 degrees and push it again.

Now, all you Dads with muscles can show how strong you are by taking the rind and squeezing out, you know, another 3 gallons of liquid from each grapefruit.

You should watch to make sure no seeds fall in. If you have a little strainer you can put that underneath the flow of liquid.

Cantaloupe:

Put your finger on the top and leave it there. Do not rotate it. Have the child cut through the fruit.

You have to scoop out the inside using a tablespoon, a bigger spoon, or anything else you want. Deposit the seeds in the trash, or save some for planting.

Cut the halves in half. Then cut each quarter into three sections.

Take one of the sections, which is a what?

$$1/4 \times 1/3 = 1/12\text{th}$$

and make five or six vertical cuts.

Now take the knife and run it close to the rind. The pieces will fall out easily, preferably into a bowl and not onto the kitchen floor.

Dates and raisins:

Dates and raisins add texture and chewiness to fruit salad. This effect may or may not be wanted, especially if your child has braces.

Watermelon:

If your child is into watermelon, that becomes a little more challenging, especially if you have watermelon with seeds.

I would suggest that you spend the extra money and get the seedless watermelons. They really are not seedless, there are just less seeds and the seeds are small, they are white, and they are very swallowable or chewable.

While the act of filling one's lungs to capacity helps to develop the diaphragm muscles, when a child fills his or her lungs it usually means that something is about to be launched into the air. The launch apparatus usually involves the lips and mouth.

When eating watermelon the projectile is usually a watermelon seed.

The usual target is another child.

You can use this opportunity to discuss the physics of flight.

Four forces work on everything that becomes airborne. I am, of course, assuming the activity is taking place on earth.

> **Thrust:** Provided by the lung full of air.
> **Drag:** Provided by air molecules through which the seed must pass before striking the intended target.
> **Lift:** Provided by the aerodynamic structure of the seed, if any.
> **Gravity:** Provided by earth and which causes all projectiles to have a parabolic curve, like the lengthwise curve of a football.

So if you want to stop a seed spitting war or "competition." Just sit the child(ren) down and start talking about physics.

Most likely they will say "This is no fun if we have to learn stuff. We'll stop spitting seeds if you stop lecturing us."

Bananas:

If your child likes bananas, I would suggest taking a banana and cutting it up on each serving instead of adding them to the mix.

Bananas turn brown/black very rapidly in air. Bananas actually pull all the pollution out of the air — only kidding.

After a day or so in the refrigerator a banana does not look very appealing. Get it, "peeling". Ha, Ha, Ha!

Lemon:

Lemons do not need to be cut in any particular way. Just cut in half and squeeze its liquid to add a little tartness to the fruit salad. (Lemon juice also helps keep fruits from browning.)

Strawberries and Raspberries:

If you have strawberries (some people are allergic to strawberries) remember to wash them very well (not "good").

That's what the colander is for. The strawberries, raspberries, white grapes or red grapes should be put in a colander and put under running, cold water. All of these fruits get a kagillion doses of pesticides, fungicides, herbicides and everything else you can think of. They all can grow fungi and molds, the white, furry kind, so wash them very well and throw away any affected fruit.

Grapes:

With red and white grapes, it is best to buy the ones without seeds. Otherwise, you have to cut them apart and remove the seeds. This may be more tedious and time-consuming than you or your child may want to do. (Definitely more tedious than this Dad can take.)

Cherries:

Cherries always have a pit in them. Cherry pitters can be fun for the child to use.

What you do is put the cherries on top of the pitter in a little indentation. There is a little plunger. The child can push the plunger. A cylinder of metal goes through the cherry and forces the pit into the jar. The plunger has a spring that returns it to its original position to accept another cherry. The pitted cherry can go into the salad.

As an aside, when I bought this little tool, T. J. spent more time pitting cherries than eating them. He told me he really didn't like cherries, he just liked pitting them.

Apples:

If you want to go to the extra expense or effort to find it, there is a thing called an apple corer. When the child cranks the handle, the mechanical devices work together. The apple is peeled, cored, and cut it into something that looks like a slinky.

A child who is shorter than 30 inches high can put an apple on this device and hand crank it. He or she can then hold up one end and the other end will reach his or her foot.

An apple which is approximately 3 inches in diameter can extend to about 3 feet.

Section 3 - Dinner

The Procession

Stuffed Potatoes

Ingredients:

1 stick	Butter
Some	Meat
1 cup	Milk
1 per person	Potatoes

Tools:

Cookie or pizza pan
Masher
Microwave
Pan
Stove with oven
Spatula
Tablespoon
Tin foil

Nothing is ever simple.

Take the potato. There are two kinds of potatoes: the white kind, that come from Idaho or Ireland and the red kind, that comes from Mars the "red planet."

The red potatoes are usually smaller and are sweeter. Because of the sweetness factor, children prefer red potatoes. Actually the Martians are preparing us for their takeover of earth just like the Russians when they were using fluoridation to take over the United States, remember?

Red potatoes also have thinner skins. We want the child to eat the potato skins. The inner layer of the potato skin contains most of the vitamins and nutrients in the potato. See, you have just learned some plant physiology that you can pass onto the child.

Basically we are going to cook a potato until it is soft. Scoop out the softened white inside, also referred to as "guts". Mix this with some kind of cooked meat, hamburger in this case, and a small amount of butter and milk, and then put the stuff back into the potato skins. We will then bake the top of the potato. Finally, the child can put grated cheese on top.

First: Wash your hands.

Then wash the potatoes. **DO NOT USE HAND SOAP TO WASH THE POTATOES.** When you "wash" vegetables, you should scrub the potatoes under running water. This scrubbing is needed, theoretically, to get rid of dirt and any chemicals that may be hanging on the surface.

Face it, potatoes are dirty. They were taken from their homes underneath the ground. You need to get the dirt off before you eat them. There is an old-wives tale that goes "You will eat a pound of dirt before your die." But. Hey. Why eat it all at one meal??

My son heard that potatoes explode.

We decided to test this hypothesis.

> **Hypothesis** - a guess by a child to get Dad to do something that seems foolish so that Dad can be blamed or, at least, Dad has to clean up the mess.

We took a small potato, about two inches in diameter, as our "Exploder." He wrapped it in white paper toweling. The white paper is supposed to make the heating more even. We set the microwave timer for 20 minutes, eight to 15 minutes is the usual time to cook an average sized potato. At approximately 15 minutes we could see smoke in the oven. I stopped the experiment by opening the oven.

The potato had not exploded. T. J. unwrapped the potato and cut it in half. The inside had been completely cooked away. It resembled a puff ball fungus. The smoke was from the paper that had reached its kindling temperature (kindling temperature - the temperature at which something bursts into flames).

We have now learned the following:
    1) Potatoes do not necessarily explode.
    2) A microwave oven, as compared to a match, is a very expensive way to burn paper toweling.
    3) The definition of kindling temperature.

Back to the recipe.

Now that the potatoes are clean, prick them three or four times with a fork. These holes prevent the potatoes from exploding (as if they could).

Then wrap them in paper towels.

We chose four potatoes and set the time for 15 minutes.

Put 1/4 cup of hamburger for each potato in a frying pan.

Start cooking the hamburger. Turn the temperature control 2/3 of the way to "High." Use a long handled spatula to turn the meat.

If there is a lot of fat in your burger this fat will go to liquid and spatter up and over the frying pan. Make sure your child has a long, long handled stirrer/spatula, this will reduce the probability of grease burns. Besides, leaner meat is better for you.

Never let the child put their face over the frying pan to "smell" the hamburger. This can result in facial burns.

Get a small bowl. This will be used to hold the insides of the potatoes and hamburger so that they can be mashed together with milk and butter.

When the microwave signals it is done, gently squeeze each potato. If they are not soft, put three more minutes on the timer and cook longer. Repeat until the potatoes are soft. Children will eat anything hard from the "Candy" food-group, but not hard potatoes from the "Vegetable" food-group.

When the potatoes are done, take them out of the microwave and unwrap them. Don't throw the paper toweling away, it can be used later to clean up messes.

The potato will naturally lie a certain way. Take a knife and cut each parallel to the surface it is on.

Scoop out the inside of the potato with a tablespoon. (The tablespoon is the large spoon that looks like the teaspoon. The teaspoon is the small spoon that looks like the tablespoon. Understand??)

Put the potato "guts", the hamburger, 1/2 cup of milk and a teaspoon (not tablespoon) of butter in the bowl.

Let your child mash the heck out of it. Just make sure most of the food remains in the bowl — or use the paper toweling as necessary.

When the gruel is sufficiently mixed, spoon the mixture back into the potato skins. Remember the hamburger increased the volume of the potato so the potato and meat mixture will be in the form of mounds.

Now put the stuffed potato skins on a cookie sheet or pizza pan. (I always cover the pan with tin foil first, so that I do not to have clean it later.)

Now we get to use the oven.

Open the oven — the big door in front. There are shelves in the oven that can be adjusted by placing the shelf in the strange metal bumpages on the side. Pick any shelf and remove it. Place this shelf as high as possible.

We are going to "broil" the top of the potatoes so that they are brownish, like a toasted marshmallow.

If your child does not like "toasted", put the potatoes back in the microwave and set the time for three (3) minutes. Skip over the next few paragraphs.

When the shelf is secure, place the pan of potatoes on the top shelf.

Do not shut the door. You need to be able to see when the top is brownish. The tinted glass in the oven window does not allow a clear view of the "toasting" process.

Set the oven dial to "Broil" and the temperature to 400 degrees. Sit back and watch.

When the potatoes look "toasted", turn the oven off, completely open the door and pull out the shelf. Use a cooking mitt or thick folded cloth when you grab the shelf or you will get burned. You should do this, not the child - no, not get burned, pull out the shelf.

Take a teaspoon and make a little dimple on the top of each potato mound. Into the dimple put some butter. Use the grater to grate cheese on the top. Salt and pepper and serve.

Personally, I like to put gravy on the potatoes. If you have left over turkey or roast beef, and the respective gravies, that is the best in my opinion. If you have really large potatoes (usually white) you can also put peas into the mixture. Then you will have a "complete meal in the skins."

Ingredients:

4-5 slices per fish	Bacon
1 per person	Fish
1/4 cup per fish	Red onions (3-4" dia., cut in 1/4" slices)
	Salt and pepper

Tools:

Barbecue Rack
Fork
Knife or Dissecting Kit
Pair of pliers (2)

Others:

Aluminum foil
Band-Aids®
Charcoal briquettes
Newspaper
Paper towels

Time: One-half hour if the coals are hot.

I want to start out talking about fishing.

Most children are interested in fishing.

Even the smallest pan fish can be a big deal to a child. The first fish T. J. caught was when he was four years old. When he picked the bluegill up, the dorsal (top) fin speared his left hand.

So here is a child — blood dripping off his left hand and a fish in his right hand.

He did not cry. He was so interested in "his" first fish.

About once a month, T. J. and his friend(s) go fishing. On one particular outing we had four parents, and seven children.

I guess we sort of cheated. We went to a rainbow trout farm in the mountains where the probability of catching a fish is approximately 100%. Fish range from one to four pounds. The price is $2.40 per pound. A fishing license is not required and you even get a "Transportation Permit" to take with you to show to the game warden if they stop you. Great fun.

All the children caught fish (see photo). The first child caught a fish on the first cast. The last, with the help and advice of the others caught his fish an hour and one-half later !!!

Photo by R.J. Turner

Seven very proud children and four parents go trout fishing.

They are (left to right): 1st row; T. J. Turner, Ryan Gatterdam, John Massale, Nils Wagner, Andy Headley, Nick Headley: 2nd Row; John Massale, Sr., Jeanne Wagner, Ila Wagner, and Ty Headley.

Preparing to cook the fish.

When we returned home, we had to prepare the fish.

T. J. and I do not clean fish. We dissect fish.

> Dissect - to cut apart piece by piece, as a body for purposes of study.

I bought a dissecting kit and a book on dissecting when T. J. was six. We have been dissecting ever since. My wife was initially very concerned about the use of a scalpel. I told T. J. about the dangers of blood-born diseases and the importance of cleaning the instruments after each use. He also knew he had to do exactly as I showed him.

I strongly suggest the following:

Seven Piece Dissecting Kit - Economy Model
    scalpel (chose disposable blade),
    scissors,
    tweezers,
    section lifter,
    dissecting needle,
    six dissecting pins, and
    glass eye dropper
all in a vinyl storage pouch.
Order No. **S31,191**, approximately $15.

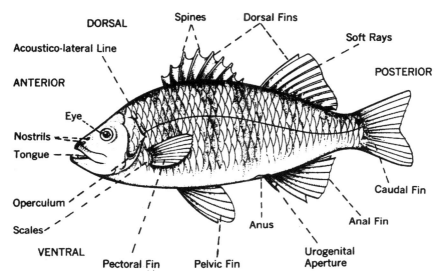

Figure 71. External Anatomy of the Perch: *Perca flavescens*.

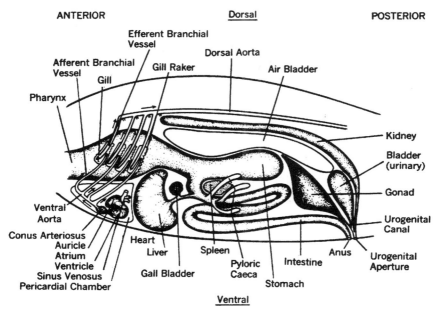

Figure 73. Internal Organs of Bony Fish: The Perch.

How to Dissect (paper back) by William Berman (214 pages).

Order No. **S9726**, approximately $10.

Both of these can be obtained from the following.

>Edmund Scientific Company
>101 East Gloucester Pike
>Barrington, NJ 08007-1380
>   To Order: (609) 547-8880

T. J. and Richie dissect a "Golden" trout. A golden trout is an albino rainbow trout, introduced from Germany and used by the state of West Virginia to celebrate its bicentennial.

Photo by R.J. Turner

Richie is going to dissect his 13-inch rainbow trout. He did not want to dissect his 15 inch rainbow trout. He is in negotiations with his father to have the trout mounted. Negotiations are needed because in our area a mounted fish goes for $5 per inch. T. J. has a mounted, 18-inch, 2-1/4 pound large mouth bass he caught when he was eight.

Spread out the newspaper.

The fish should be held on its back with its stomach up. (You should help hold the fish.) An incision is made from the anal hole, near the tail, to the head so that the internal organs can be removed.

With a knife stick the point into the anal hole and using a sawing motion work the knife slowly to the head.

With a scalpel, use short stroking motions with increasing pressure as the skin and muscles are cut. The scalpel should be held like a pencil with the index finger extended and on the handle. The finger should apply pressure during the cutting stroke. Only the rounded portion of the scalpel should be used for cutting — **Never the point.**

Once the fish has been cut open, it can be turned on the side. The knife/scalpel can be used to remove the organs. If you have the dissecting book, or one from the library, or maybe in the future www.dissect.com, you can show your knowledge of biology to your child.

The stomach is particularly interesting. A fish caught in the wild will have what it has eaten most recently. This will help you catch more of the same type fish in the same location later or the same time next year.

Once the internal organs are removed, you will see a dark area up against the backbone. This is blood and needs to be removed. Take the knife/scalpel and cut the membrane housing the blood. Then, use the knife/scalpel to clean out the blood.

You can choose to leave the head on or cut it off (see "skinning" below). If you decide to cut the head off, you need to take the knife/scalpel and cut behind the front side fins (pectoral fin) near the gills. Cut on one side and then flip the fish over and cut on the other side. The child may need help cutting through the backbone.

I would leave the skin on for barbecuing. Once cooked the skin is easier to remove. Also, if the fish are less than 10 inches long a large amount of meat may be removed during the skinning process.

Unlike other fish, trout do not have scales. If you do not have a trout, you will need to scale or skin the fish.

Scaling

Scaling can be accomplished with a scaler, if you have one. I just use a knife. Hold the blade perpendicular to the body of the fish. Hold the head with your hand or a pair of pliers. Start at the tail and bring the flat side of the knife toward you. This will dislodge the scales.

The child will be interested in helping. He/she will find that by pulling the knife rapidly toward him/her the scales will fly to great heights and distance from the newspaper — so be ready for a mess.

Every inch of the fish should be scaled. Eating a scale is like eating cellophane; most children will reject the fish if they bite down on a scale. I even run a knife blade over trout.

Skinning

This is more difficult and, except for catfish and eels, requires strength. You will need to cut through the skin along the back bone of the fish. Unless you have "one hell of a grip" you will need two pairs of pliers. Skinning is easier to do with the fish's head still on.

Hold the head with one pair of pliers. With the other pair take hold of the skin near the head and the backbone. You may need to cut into the meat with the knife to get a good grip. Now pull the skin off in the direction of the tail. Repeat this process on the other side.

Now, clean the fish (outside and the inside) under cold running water.

Finally, the recipe.

Well, not quite. You have to have the barbecue grill ready. If you are using charcoal briquettes they should be white hot.

Cut the skin off the onion. Position the onion so that the top, where the green stuff grew out, is under your thumb. Now cut down through the onion ... not your thumb.

Put the two halves on the flat side. The onion should be cut in slices of approximately 1/4 inch slices.

If you do the cutting, your eyes may start watering.

Or, you can have the child cut the onion.

You have to explain that raw onions give off a gas that will cause their eyes to burn and to water or "cry."

We veterans can recount those memorable times we were introduced to CS gas during basic training.

Tell the child this "crying" is a temporary condition. However, the experience will be remembered by children to be used later when there are important and substantial negotiations with parents.

The stomach cavity of the fish should be salted and peppered. Then, the slices of onion are put into the stomach cavity. The onion will provide moisture and flavoring as the fish cooks.

The fish now needs to be completely wrapped with bacon slices. The wrapping should be done in a continuous fashion. Start at the head or tail. At the end of one piece of bacon overlap the next piece. It will take four or five strips for a 12 inch fish, if the fish is fat it will take more. The reason the wrapping should be tight and overlapped is that bacon shrinks when it is cooked.

To grill, I like to use a hamburger holder. (Wal-Mart®, approximately $15.)

Fish do not take long to cook. You have to watch them.

If flames leap up from the bacon fat, you should sprinkle water on the coals to cool them. You want to keep the heat low and even. (Don't splash water on hot coals or you will be eating grainy bits of charcoal with your fish!)

When the bacon starts to crisp and the fish begins to "flake," (check with a fork) — the meat should pull apart easily — the fish(es) is/are done.

> **HINT:** If you start eating the meat from the tail first, there is a lower probability of bone. As you come toward the head (about half-way up the fish), start eating the meat from the rib cage. The upper quadrant near the head will have very small bones. Nothing spoils a fishing/cooking experience more than a bone in the throat.

WATCH THE CHILDREN EATING FISH CAREFULLY.

Barbecued Chicken:

Ingredients:

    Chicken
    Catsup
    Barbecue sauce
    Spices (or at least salt and pepper)

Tools:

    Grill
    Tongs, long handle
    Fork, long handle
    Basting brush (or 1" or 2" paint brush - clean)
    Knives
    Meat cutting saw (or hacksaw - clean)
    Poultry scissors (or tin snips - clean)

Preparing the chicken:

For the more adventurous of those among you, and if you have the proper equipment, buy a whole chicken. It is a lot more exciting to prepare a whole chicken to barbecue than to buy the pieces.

When buying a whole chicken, you get to cut it up using various tools. There are "proper" meat cutting tools like poultry scissors, or, if you happen to have them, you can use a hacksaw and tin snips.

The machete and hatchet are not tools-of-the-trade in the culinary art. However, they are interesting utensils not necessarily to be used on counter tops with ceramic or terra-cotta tile.

> **Caution:** If you have an old chopping block and the child would like to take a whack with the machete, at least this is sort of safe, because for most children it takes two hands to hold the machete. So, say, you lay a fish down and they say oh, let's cut off its head, you can say sure and use the machete or the hatchet to do that.

When preparing to barbecue chicken, the first thing you have to do is clean out the inside of the chicken. If you bought your chicken in a grocery store, you'll find there is a bag of "innards" inside the chicken. Innards are things that used to be "In nard" chicken — like, the heart, the liver and the gizzards.

> **NOTE:** Unlike human beings that have enzymes and bacteria that help us digest our food, most fowl have gizzards. Gizzards grind up food in the fowl.

These "innards," which are also called giblets, can be cooked a number of ways.

We like to boil them in a pot of water or fry them in the frying pan with a little butter and onions. In any case, all three innards have different consistencies, textures and tastes, that your child may or may not like.

The heart, the smallest of the three, is very tender. The gizzard, shaped like a bow tie, is chewy: especially the gristle that separates the two bows of the tie. The liver is tender, but has the strongest taste.

You might as well put them in a pot of water and boil them while you are doing the rest of the meal. Just make sure that there is a lot of water in the pot. Don't forget that you are cooking them.

Once upon a time, I made the mistake of buying a package of gizzards and put them on the stove to boil. I forgot all about them. I went back three hours later and there was no water, a terrible smell, and this black residue had bonded to my Farberwear® pot. Even with a wood chisel and hammer I couldn't get "it" off the pot. Chuck that up to experience. I also chucked the pot!

Once you've cleaned the inside of the chicken, you must decide if you need to remove excess fat and/or skin.

Some people don't like skin. The easiest way to get the skin off the chicken is to pull it with your hands. Now, the problem with your hands is that your grip is a function of the pores on your hand skin. After pulling chicken skin for even a short amount of time your pores will get filled up with chicken fat.

For greater gripability, I suggest that you have a little trickle of hot water. Every now-and-then, wash your hands when your grip slips.

I would suggest putting the fat, and any other leftovers from the chicken, into air-tight bags like Ziplock® before you put it in the trash. Nothing smells worse or gets rotten faster than chicken fat.

When you have removed unwanted fat and/or skin, you are ready for the toolbox.

Take the tin snips or the hacksaw (or poultry scissors) and cut the chicken down the backbone. Then cut down through the breast. You now have two halves of the chicken.

Cut below the rib cage to separate the leg sections from breast. You now have a quartered chicken. If you need to separate drumsticks (for smaller hands and appetites) bend the leg at the joint and cut through the joint with a knife.

Preparing the barbecue sauce:

You can buy your barbecue sauce or make it yourself.

If you decide to make it, you need something that is red and something that adds taste, what we call spice.

For the red part, you can use catsup, tomato soup, tomato paste, or you can use anything with tomato. It just has to be gooey enough so that you can spread it on the chicken.

You can cut up whole tomatoes and squish them up and make the whole thing from scratch. You will need salt and pepper. You can cut up peppers and onions. You can use A-1 Steak Sauce®, Worcestershire Sauce®, or soy sauce. Any one of these three liquids will make the barbecue sauce look darker.

Barbecuing (finally!)

Now you are ready to light the fire. Light the barbecue briquettes and let them turn white before putting the meat on. You can put the meat directly on the grill **after** you clean the grill. Or, you can also use a hamburger holder that you can get at Wal-Mart®. That's probably easier for you and your child to flip over. But, it is not as exciting as taking that long fork or spatula and trying your wits against the heat coming out of the barbecue.

While the briquettes are heating up, put the meat in a bowl or pan and pour the barbecue sauce on top of it. The meat will soak up some of the sauce so the flavor remains even if it looks as if the sauce all cooks away.

Put the pieces in the hamburger flipper. I like that better because you don't lose as much meat down through the cracks in the grill, and you don't have to worry about burnt hands because the handle is long enough you can turn it over without getting anywhere near the coals. Once the meat is on the barbecue, T. J. likes to brush the meat with the sauce.

Let it cook a little while. When you flip it over, brush it with sauce again

Do it over and over again until the meat is done. "Done" is when, if you poke the chicken meat, **no** blood comes out. Unlike red meat, white meat like pork, chicken, turkey, so forth, should have a colorless juice when the meat is thoroughly cooked. There is no such thing as "medium-rare chicken." If there is blood the chicken has been cooked improperly. If you eat it, you may get sick.

Cooking a Turkey:

Why a turkey?

1) Turkey is low in fat,
2) It gives your child a choice of white or dark meat (or two other things not to like), and
3) It's big.

Ingredients:

Some	Butter
Some	Stuffing (optional)
1	Turkey

Tools:

Basting brush
Kitchen chair (You'll see what a chair has to do with cooking a turkey.)
Mop or broom
Pan, large
Stove
Two plastic shopping bags

Three factors must be considered to successfully cook a turkey.

1) Length of cooking time.
2) Temperature of the oven.
3) Weight of the turkey.

The right combination of these three will produce a moist, tasty turkey. The wrong combination can produce meat that is hard to cut, or spouts blood when cut, or is so dry that it resembles shredded-wheat meat.

It is easy enough to understand time - you need a watch or timer.

The temperature can be set with a dial for an electric stove, assuming that the thermocouples and the associated electrical circuitry works. And you can double check the setting by using an oven thermometer (oven settings are notoriously "off").

Usually the weight of the turkey is printed somewhere on its plastic wrapping. If there is no "official" weight or if the covering has been thrown away or eaten by the dog, what can you do?

You can teach the child about "weighing by differences", about using a simple tool — the lever, and mathematical modeling — a direct application of physics and linear algebra.

Weighing by Differences

If you have a bathroom scale, have the child bring it to the kitchen.

If the bathroom scale is the spring type with a semicircular viewing area, then you have to weigh by differences to get a true weight. If its a digital scale, you may not.

Springs and piezoelectric crystals are designed and engineered to perform accurately in the range 40 to 200 pounds, which is the weight of 99% of us humans. Scales are not usually calibrated accurately outside of this range. Since, I assume, your turkey does not weigh 40 pounds more or less, putting the turkey directly on the scale may not give you the correct weight.

What to do?

Have the child stand on the scale.

Write down the weight of the child.

Give the child the turkey in a shopping bag and have him/her hold it.

Record the new weight. Use simple arithmetic to calculate the turkey's weight.

$$\frac{\text{Weight of child holding turkey}}{\text{Weight of the turkey!!}} - \text{Child's weight}$$

Or you can use algebra. This is a linear algebraic problem in one unknown.

Algebra is a generalized arithmetic. Both arithmetic and algebra deal with numbers, but algebra also uses variables or "unknowns," which are represented by letters, like "x" and "y". (This permits more complicated problems to be solved.) The Hindu and Greek, developed our current system of numbers and mathematics and their works were preserved mainly by Moslem scholars. In fact, the Arabs greatly expanded on this work. Mohammed ibn musa al-Khowarizmi wrote books on algebra and on the Hindu numeration system, which is the number system we use today. One of al-Khowarizmi's most famous books was **Hisab al-jabr-wal mugabalah**. From his title we get the very word "algebra."

Let's use algebra to solve this turkey of a problem. To do that we have to develop a formula or relationship between the variables.

Let "x" = the weight of your child
Let "y" = the weight of your child with the turkey
Let "t" = the weight of the turkey.

Then we can write the following formula

$$t = y - x$$

Let's say your child weights 70 pounds. The weight of your child holding the turkey is 80 pounds. Then,

$x = 70$

$y = 80$

Putting these numerical values into the "formula" (called substituting) gives you.

$t = 80 - 70 = 10$ pounds

This is called weighing by difference: the difference between x and y pounds.

You have no scale. Then what?

Weighing using Physics and a Simple Machine

We will use physics to find the weight of the turkey. In particular, we will use a simple machine as a tool — a lever and a fulcrum as a first class lever. This can be most easily visualized as a see-saw. Yep, this is fun!

Use a broom or mop as the lever. Use the back of a kitchen chair as the fulcrum.

Have your child hold out an index finger. Move the handle of the broom or mop until it is balanced on his or her finger.

This is called the balance point. This indicates that the weight on the right side of the finger (the fulcrum) equals the weight on the left side of the finger.

Mark the handle at this point.

Now, get the two shopping bags.

Get a lot of large and small cans of food.

Put a cloth or pot holder over the back of a chair. This reduces the possibility of the broom/mop slipping.

Position the mark on the broom or mop on the back of the chair. The broom or mop should still balance.

Now hang the turkey in the bag from one end of the broom or mop. At the other end hang the bag of canned goods. Take out cans or add more smaller cans until the lever is balanced.

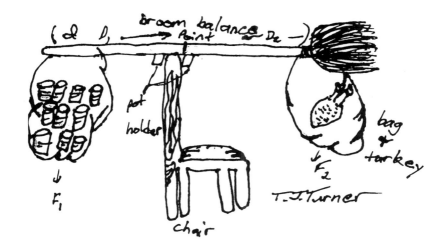

You will have to keep the mark over the back of the chair as the child adds and takes away cans.

Or if your child is old enough, or strong enough his or her index finger can be the fulcrum. Have the child hold the bag with turkey in one hand. Have him/her hold the empty bag in the other hand. Now start filling the bag with canned goods. The child's brain will use input from his/her nervous system in his/her hand and arm muscles to calculate an equilibrium point — the point when the turkey in the bag "feels" equal to the cans in the bag.

If you thought this was a lot of work you are absolutely correct.

$$\text{Work} = \text{Force} \times \text{Distance}$$

$$\text{Force} \times \text{Distance} = \text{Force} \times \text{Distance}$$

Measure the length of the lever from the turkey bag to the mark. Now, measure the length of the lever from the canned goods bag to the mark.

After the broom or mop is balanced, take the canned goods out.

Have the child write down the weight of each can in a column. By adding up the can weights, you will have the weight of the cans. Certainly good enough for government work!

We now have all the data we need to solve an algebraic problem to obtain the weight of the turkey. You need only set up an algebraic formula based on physics.

First we need to define our variables.

Force = Turkey = ???
Distance = inches to the fulcrum
Force = Weight of the cans
Distance = inches to the fulcrum

Example:
Force = Turkey
Distance = 36 in.
Force = 20 pounds
Distance = 12 in.

Turkey x 36 in. = 20 pounds x 12 ins.

$$Turkey = \frac{20 \times 12}{36} = 10 \text{ pounds}$$

You have learned about
- physics,
- simple machines, lever and fulcrum,
- a principle of physics;
  - work = force x distance,
- formed a mathematical model of a problem,
- used algebra to solve a linear equation in one unknown, and
- did some math.

You **REALLY** must be hungry by now.

Temperature and Time:

The following is a table of ranges of the various heats and times as a function of weight for a turkey according to **Turkey All Year** by Susan O. Byrne and Barbara M. Mueller (Barclay-Ramsel Associates, P.O. Box 7122 Arlington, VA 22207) p.8.

ROASTING CHART
(An unstuffed turkey baked at 325° in an uncovered roasting pan)

Weight	Hours Cooking	Resting
5-8 pounds	3 - 4 hrs.	20 minutes
8-12 pounds	3 1/2 - 4 1/2 hrs.	20-30 minutes
12-16 pounds	3 1/2 - 4 1/2 hrs.	20-30 minutes
16-20 pounds	4 - 6 1/4 hrs.	30 minutes
20-24 pounds	5 - 7 1/4 hrs.	30 minutes

> **NOTE:** Add 20 minutes total to the roasting times for stuffed turkeys up to 12 pounds. For stuffed turkeys over 12 pounds, use the regular roasting chart.

> **NOTE:** You cannot cook a 10 pound turkey in 15 minutes at 1,000 degrees and expect to eat it. With similar distorted logic, do you want to wait 18 hours to cook a 10 pound turkey at 25 degrees??

Before you put the turkey in the oven you can put stuffing or peeled and cleaned vegetables into the body cavity of the turkey. Stuffing is a world unto itself. I suggest just buying Stove Top Stuffing® and read the simple directions (essentially, just add water.)

Now put the turkey in the oven.

Basting

During the cooking process, you need to "baste" the turkey. This is the process of sucking the liquid that cooks out of the turkey and then putting it back onto the turkey. Basting keeps the turkey moist. This process should occur approximately every 30 to 60 minutes. The child will want to squeeze the basting thing — that rubber ball at the end — and watch the liquid go up the tube.

> **CAUTION:** This is hot fat. It will cause severe burns. The child should be closely supervised.

ALTERNATIVE: Forget the math and physics and just buy a ButterBall® turkey and watch for the plastic thing-a-ma-jig to pop out when the turkey is done.

You can also check if the turkey is done by brute force. If the drumsticks are easily separated from the bone, the turkey is done.

Let the turkey stand (set on the counter) for 15 to 20 minutes. Carve the turkey. Feast.

I'll spare you a biology lesson on the anatomy of the turkey. You're entirely welcome.

Foil Supper

This is a favorite to Boy Scouts and Cub Scouts on camp outs because it is:

1) easy to make,
2) goof-proof, and
2) tastes good.

What you do is essentially steam cook vegetables and meat together over an open fire or in the coals that are left after the flames die down.

You can also use this recipe in any dwelling unit that has a fire place or barbecue. All you need is fire and coals.

Ingredients:

Cabbage	
Carrots	
Celery	if you like
Meat	Hamburger or chuck roast; if it's a piece of meat it should be cut into small pieces.
Peas	if you like it
Potato	
Salt and pepper.	

Tools:

Knife
Tongs
Tin foil
Fire (Yes! Fire is a tool.)

Take a roll of tin or aluminum foil and tear off a piece about 2 feet long. In the center of the foil, put in two or three leaves of cabbage, this forms the base. The leaves sort of make a bowl shape.

Take carrots and clean and peel them. Cut them into slices about one-quarter inch thick.

Take potatoes and clean them. You should leave the skin on since the vitamins and nutrients are in the layer of skin. You should slice the potatoes in quarter inch thick slices.

Put a layer of vegetables onto the cabbage leaves.

Either use hamburger or other kinds of meat. If it is some other kinds of meat, you should cut it into thin slices or small chunks (1 inch x 1 inch). Hamburgers you should make into patties.

Now put the meat on top of the vegetables.

You may want to add some salt and pepper or Mrs. Dash®.

Close the tin foil up very tight. If you are not using "heavy duty" tin foil, get another piece out and double wrap it.

Now put this into the fire. Don't punch any holes in it. If you do have holes in the foil they will let the juices drip out. If it is fatty meat, the flames will shoot up and it may be dangerous.

When it cooks, the juices all run together and the vegetables get soft and tasty.

Usually you should leave it in the fire a half an hour to an hour. If you forget about it, that's okay too, it will still be all right. I, of course, don't mean to forget all about it and the next morning start another fire on top of it. But, in most cases it doesn't matter how long you cook it.

When you take it out, you have to be very careful when unfolding the tin foil because steam will escape. If a child is interested in seeing his or her culinary skills and bends over to smell it, the child could get his/her nose or face scalded from the escaping steam. Open the foil at an arms-length distance and let the contents cool off.

You can use the foil as the "plate" out of which you eat your supper. It is usually good to have a fork and a knife. Again, you may want to salt and pepper it a little more.

Remember to put out the fire. Pour water on the coals. Spread the coals out.

Take the tin or aluminum foil home with you. Do not bury it. Tin and aluminum foil do not decompose.

Section 4 - Dessert

Creative "Caking"

I am continually amazed by what I call the "inging" of nouns. This is turning an otherwise perfectly good noun into a verb. Some "ing" words have been with us as long as man/woman: e.g., hunt - hunting, fish-fishing, etc. But recently, there seems to be a rush to "ing" every noun. Some of these ingings are given credibility by school systems. There are now computer classes called keyboarding.

Anyway, I digress.

In leaving this topic, let me state that "caking" will soon be in Webster's dictionary. Also, when you finish cooking, put the dirty bowls, plates, and utensils in a dishwasher for what T. J. calls "dishing."

Ingredients:

1 stick	Butter
1 box	Chocolate cake mix
2	Eggs
3 bottles	Food coloring - red, blue and yellow
1 cup	Milk
1 cup	Sugar, powdered

Tools:

4	Bowls - one large (10 in. diameter) and three small (6 in. diameter).
2	Cake tin, rectangular, 9 in. x 13 in.
1	Cooling rack
1	Magic-Marker or crayon
1	Pair of scissors
1	Pencil
2 feet	String
2	Table knives

Cakes have been around for a long time.

There are many types of cakes — birthday cakes, wedding cakes, and anniversary cakes.

Any cookbook worth its salt, or sodium chloride, has a cake in it.

This recipe helps you make a cake into a "thing."

We became involved in this transformation when T. J.'s Cub Scout Pack decided to hold a fund raiser at their annual Blue and Gold Banquet. It was decided that the scouts and their Dads would bake cakes, and the cakes would be raffled off.

Since T. J. and I like fishing, T. J. thought we should make a "fish" cake.

This is how to make a fish cake.

Fish Cake (A big one — that didn't get away)

We had to make a fish template - a profile, pattern, or outline of a fish. He wanted a big fish. Therefore, I gave him a sheet of newspaper to draw the outline on.

Before he started I had him trace the outline of the pan we were going to use to cook the cake in. Most baking pans are rectangular. Since he wanted a BIG fish, I thought we could divide the batter in half and cook two cakes giving us more surface area. So, I had him trace the pan twice, side-by-side along the long side (see illustration, below). This gave him the outline of the area in which he could draw the fish.

Next he drew the fish on the newspaper. (We used a black, magic marker, but a crayon is just as good.)

cake pan: 9 inches wide by 13 inches long

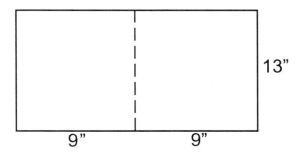

He then cut out the silhouette of the fish from the newspaper with a pair of scissors and behold — his template!

Baking

We had chosen Duncan Hines® Moist Deluxe Devil's Food® Chocolate cake mix. T. J. read the directions as I gathered the ingredients. He measured the amounts and mixed the batter.

It is very important to grease the pan well so that the cake will actually come out in one piece. We were trying to make one big fish not a school of little fish pieces.

We then filled up the pan with half the batter and put it in the oven.

> **Note:** Half a cake mix in a big pan will bake faster than printed on the box. Watch the cake carefully after 15 minutes. Stick a tooth pick in the center. If it comes out clean, the cake is done.

After the first section of the fish cake was done we turned it onto a rack to cool. Then we poured the rest of the batter in the re-greased pan and cooked the second section of the fish.

As the two cakes were cooling. I cut a piece of cardboard from a cardboard box and T. J. cut it into the size of the template outline. We used tape to put the two pieces together for what would easily be a "10 pounder."

He covered the cardboard with tinfoil, which serves several purposes:

1) it creates a clean surface to put the fish on,
2) it provides a way to carry the large fish, and
3) it makes the fish stand out.

I put the two cooled cakes on the tinfoil-covered cardboard side by side (long ways).

He placed his fish template on the two sections of cake and cut around the outline with a table knife.

> **Note:** Chocolate is a big no-no for dogs.

Decorating

T. J. wanted the fish to be green with a red eye and a black gill, tail, and fins. (See diagram on page 145.)

Butter frosting is probably the easiest frosting to make, so that is why we made it.

We used three bowls:

>one for green,
>one for red, and
>one for black.

Colors

Food coloring only comes in a limited number of colors. Therefore, I had an opportunity to discuss primary and secondary colors with T. J. All colors are a combination of the three primary colors.

In nature things usually occur in multiples of two.
For example:
>Magnetism - north and south poles
>Energy - kinetic and potential
>Thermodynamics - hot and cold.

For every action there is an opposite and equal reaction.

Flight - lift, up; gravity, down; thrust, forward; and drag, slowing.

Boolean logic - 0's and 1's, on/off.
The basis of our modern computer.

You and your child can list other phenomena here!

_____ - _____

_____ - _____

_____ - _____

_____ - _____

But man-made systems seem to come in threes! How odd.

For example:

Christianity - Father, Son, and Holy Ghost

America - mother, apple pie, and baseball.

The Greeks were into threes

Geometry - triangles; three sides.

Logic - thesis, anti-thesis, and synthesis.

Government - Executive, Legislature and Judiciary branches.

Stop light - stop, go and caution

You and your child can list other phenomenon here!

_____ - _____

_____ - _____

_____ - _____

_____ - _____

Enough philosophy.

The three primary colors are red, yellow and blue. These colors run the full length of the visible spectrum — the colors that our brain can process from the input from our optical system — our eyes. Computers, with 64-bits and output matrixes of 720x720 points can now produce over a million colors. We know this because we can calculate their existence. The problem is that we cannot actually "see" all these colors. Even if we could see these colors, who could remember all those names??? One gigantic box of Cray-o-las®.

White is the combination of all colors.

Black is the absence of all color.

Experiment:

Take a square sheet of paper. Fold it once lengthwise and then once again. This will divide the square into four equal sections. Have your child get crayons or colored pencils. Have the child color one section red, one section blue, and one section yellow. Put a pin through the center of the paper and put the pin onto an eraser of a pencil. If you spin the paper fast enough the colors will disappear and you will only see white.

If you didn't see white, tape the square or circle to a circular sander. Put the sander into your drill and turn it on. Now for sure your brain will "see" white!

This is called an "optical illusion." The colors are still on the paper but you have tricked your brain into using one of your five senses: sight, i.e., the optic nerve!

This experiment is more dramatic if you use only the three colors of equal size and a circle. But, that would require a protractor to make the 120 degree angles as shown below.

You can make many colors from the primary colors depending on the amount of color used. Just as the points of a compass are north, south, east and west there are directions in between like northeast, northwest, southeast and southwest as shown below.

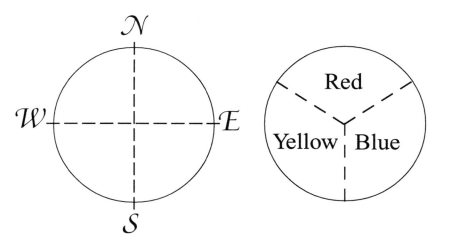

The primary colors have colors in between
    yellow and blue - green
    blue and red - purple
    red and yellow - orange

T. J. wanted

    1) green, a mixture of yellow and blue
    2) red, a primary color; and
    3) black, a mixture; blue with a touch of red.

The green frosting covers the portion where the two layers were connected.

If you are not into fishing, but coach - soccer, football, baseball, volleyball, you can make a ball cake, bat cake, goal cake, puck cake, etc.

Ball Cake:

To make a ball cake, cut a piece of string the length of the shorter side of the cake pan.

Since

Diameter = 2 x Radius

Take hold of both ends of the string in one of your hands. Now hold the ends of string in the approximate center of the cake. Have the child place a pencil in the loop of the string. Then with you holding tight at the center, have the child pull against the string, while moving the pencil left or right. The force pulling the pencil into an arc is centripetal force. The child is applying centrifugal force. The curve made by the child is an arc. An arc of 360 degrees is a circle - the profile of a ball. (A circle is two dimensional, a ball is three dimensional.)

Use this method to make the cardboard for the base and to make the cake.

See math can be fun. Even if you cannot get the right answer here, at least you can eat the problem.

If you are not into geometry, physics, or hand-eye coordination then, just buy a round cake tin. But, string is less expensive and more exciting.

According to Bruce Nash and Allan Zullo's book
Sports Hall of Shame, Golf Cartoon Classics
(Tribune Publishing, Orlando, FL, 1993)

Janice Irby provided a birthday blast for her golf-fanatic husband John by slipping several golf balls into his cake before putting it into the oven. John will never forget the day in 1987 when he turned 30 – because the heated balls exploded, shooting cake all over the oven and sending the smell of burning rubber throughout the Irby's home...

Cookies

Cookie Skyscraper

Oreo® cookies by Nabisco® have been around since forever. They are an institution in themselves.

This a simple takeoff on the Oreo®-like cookie. This recipe is good in the summer or the winter.

Ingredients:

1 box or bag	Chocolate cookies
1 cup	Sugar
2 teaspoons	Vanilla Extract
1 half pint	Whipping cream, (the little carton) heavy **(Check the date on carton)**

Tools:

1	Beater, electric (cold beaters, put in refrigerator) or hand beater.
1	Bowl (cold, put in refrigerator)
1	Spoon

I will also introduce your child to masonry skills: the use of mortar (whipped cream) to hold cookies together.

Jokes

Question: What is black and white and read all over?
Answer: A newspaper.

or

Question: What is black and white and red all over.
Answer: A chocolate ice cream soda with ketchup.
Oh, Yuck!!!

This recipe is better than the jokes.

Whipped Cream:

The firmness of the whipped cream will be better; i.e., thicker, if the bowl — and the beaters — are cold. For this reason I like to use a metal mixing bowl. I put the bowl and beaters in the freezer for an hour before I use them. But, if this is a spur-of-the-moment project, grab anything.

Pour the cream into the bowl. Add three teaspoons (yes, the little spoon) of sugar. Add one teaspoon of vanilla extract.

Use the electric beater **AT THE WHIP SETTING** to whip the cream.

> **CAUTION** - if you let the child hold the beater, tell him/her to keep the beaters in the cream. If he or she decides to lift the beaters up above the edge of the bowl, the whipping cream gets really excited about the possibility of escaping the bowl. It rushes with great speed to attach itself to every surface in the kitchen, including the ceiling.

The cream is sufficiently whipped when you can take a spoonful and when the spoon is lifted slowly from the bowl the surface of the whipped cream forms a point, i.e., peak, that does not go back to a level surface in the bowl for three minutes. Be careful not to over whip — it becomes butter-like and won't taste like whipped cream. If the spoon stays straight up and down in the whipped cream it is over whipped.

Now you simply take a cookie and place a teaspoon, or two, of whipped cream on it.

Now put another cookie on the top.

Ta-Dah, you're building a Cookie Skyscraper.

You can continue the process to make any number of levels

>> double - 2
>> triple - 3
>> quadruple - 4
>> quintuple - 5, etc.

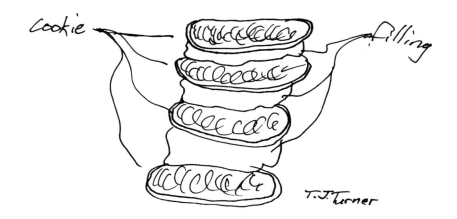

Increase your vocabulary while feeding your face.

Put the skyscrapers into the freezer and leave for an hour. This firms the cream and makes it "ice cream-like."

Just eat them frozen with your fingers.

On hot days these are cooling.

On cold days make hot chocolate and dunk the Cookie Skyscraper into the hot chocolate. They cool the chocolate drink and add lots of melted whipped cream.

If you want to be festive, get a number of bowls and add your child's favorite color to the cream before it is whipped. The colored whipped cream make festive looking "logs" or "loaves" for parties and special occasions.

Sort-of Rice Crispie® Treats

Minnesota Manufacturing and Mining Company, known as 3M, started out with a good bonding mixture. They invented glue, essentially. They did not know exactly what to do with it. They decided well, if we spread this on paper and sprinkle sand on it we can call it sandpaper. That's how 3M® got started.

What we are going to do is re-invent, no not the wheel, but sandpaper.

We are going to take marshmallows and use them to bond Rice Crispies® together.

Ingredients:

    1 stick   Butter
    1 bag   Marshmallows, small
    1 box   Rice Crispies®

Tools:

Chisel (in case you fail at making this recipe and want to rescue the pan.)
Knife
Pan
Stirrer

We need to melt the marshmallows. This isn't hard because they melt very easily. Put marshmallows into a little pot, warm it up.

If you want to do something inventive, you could of course add food coloring to the melted marshmallows.

Go back to the caking recipe and read the part about how to mix whatever color you want and put it in the adhesive part of the marshmallows.

In the meantime you can take some butter and melt it. Put the pan on another unit of the stove and put butter in it. When the butter melts, swish it around so that when you pour the concoction into the pan you can get it out.

Once you mix the Rice Crispies® and marshmallow goo together you need to put the pan in the refrigerator to cool the solution down and/or to speed up the bonding process.

Once the pan has stayed in the refrigerator for a short time, say one hour, you can take it out.

Cut up the bonded mass.

Hope you can get it out of the pan.

Ice Cream Things

<u>Humdinger</u>

This is really a tall (vertical) banana split.

Regular banana splits are from the horizontal food group (horizontal meaning level with the earth's surface — flat). A Humdinger is from the vertical food group (vertical means it is perpendicular to the earth's surface — tall).

Four-layer chocolate birthday cakes are from the vertical food group. If you drop a piece of birthday cake on the floor, it now belongs to the horizontal food group.

Ingredients:

1 per serving	Bananas
1 pint each	Ice cream
	Vanilla,
	Chocolate
	Strawberry
Some	Maraschino cherries
1 cup	Milk
Some	Nuts
1 can	Soda - root beer,
	7-Up, Coke®
Small Jars	Topping
	Chocolate
	Pineapple
	Strawberry

	(Toppings cont.)
	Butterscotch
	Jams and jellies
1 can	Whipped cream (already prepared is the simplest: Redi-Whip® or Dream Whip®)

Tools:

Glass or mug, tall
Ice cream scoop
Plastic drink cup; 20 to 32 oz.
Spoon - long handle
Table knife

The customary banana fencing dual should be fought before peeling the bananas. Then have your child peel the banana(s).

Have your child use a table knife to cut the bananas in slices lengthwise. The slices should be thin; about 1/4 inches.

Yes! The chef(s) can sample the banana.

Let the layering begin!

1) Put in the glass or mug a layer of ice cream, say, vanilla.

2) Put in a layer of banana slices, like, 1/3 of a banana.

3) Add a layer of topping/jelly, say, pineapple or marmalade.

4) Next a layer of ice cream, like, chocolate.

5) Put in another layer of banana slices, like, 1/3 of a banana.

6) Add another layer of topping.

7) One more layer of ice cream, like, strawberry.

8) Now a layer of banana slices.

9) And, last, a layer of topping, like, chocolate.

10) Finally, whipped cream.

11) Nuts

12) Top off with a Maraschino cherry.

    T. J. likes to put in some type of soda. The soda crystallizes some of the outside of the ice cream and gives an interesting texture.

> **Note:** Do not use tonic water. It will taste terrible.

Putting in some milk helps to thaw the ice cream and makes the flavors mix together.

If the child cannot finish the Humdinger, just put it in the freezer. When he/she wants it again, just put it in the microwave oven and set for 20 to 30 seconds on high.

> **Caution:** Although Humdingers are great after strenuous athletic events, they should not be the first thing to enter the body. Always have one or two glasses of water first. You need time to get re-hydrated; i.e., replace the water lost through sweat and your body needs to regulate its temperature and heart rate. Marathon runners can reach body temperatures of over 104 degrees!! Taking ice cream into a hot body can cause vomiting or an "ice cream" headache. The thermostat in your brain cannot handle the abrupt temperature change.

If there are more than four children preparing a Humdinger, it is probably not smart to have the pressurized type of whipped cream. It seems these cans each send irresistible messages to children, like — "Hey buddy. Your friend would sure look good with whipped cream on his/her head." On the other hand, if you are outside on a hot summer day in swim suits, near a pool, or have a garden hose handy what the heck!

If you really want to live dangerously make an ice cream mountain. This is essentially a Humdinger built in a bowl.

Milk Shake

Ingredients:

    Ice Cream   Vanilla, chocolate, coffee, strawberry, just about any flavor

    Milk

    Soda   Root beer, Coca Cola®, seltzer water. Not tonic water or grape soda.

Tools:

    Electric beater/electric drill
    Glass
    Spoon, iced tea
    Tablespoon

Put the ice cream into the glass with the tablespoon. Do not pack the ice cream down with the spoon. You want to maximize the surface area of the ice cream so that the largest amount of liquids comes in contact with the ice cream.

You can put in layers of different types of ice cream. There is no "wrong" way of putting ice cream in the glass – no matter what the sibling says.

Fill about 2/3 of the glass with ice cream. Do not fill more than 3/4 of the glass with ice cream.

Now pour in the soda.

If the soda is warm, as the warm liquid hits the cold ice cream the carbonation will be released in the form of bubbles. When you cool a liquid that has gas molecules between the molecules of liquid the space between the liquid molecules decreases and squeezes out the carbonation molecules.

This physical reaction will cause small ice crystals to form on the ice cream and add to the texture of the milkshake.

Pour in the soda until the bubbles are level with the top of the glass.

Now pour in the milk. The milk will fill up the area that was filled with the bubbles. Some of the bubbles may (will) come out of the glass and spill down the side. Just use toweling to clean up the spill.

Use the long handled spoon to gently stir the mixture.

If the child is small, you should hold the glass. If you do not hold the glass, the vertical drink may become a horizontal mess, especially if the ice cream decides to grab hold of the spoon and the child decides to fight the mean ice cream glob.

If you really want to be able to drink the mixture through a straw, you have a couple of options.

1) **Put the contents of the glass into a container that can be used in a microwave.** The glass may have its crystal structure affected by the cold solution. Therefore, it may break when exposed to the microwave's frequency.

Heat in the microwave oven for 20 seconds. This sort of defeats the objective of "ice" cream, but does speed up the mixing and melting process.

2) Use a beater. **Do not use the glass.** The beater may break the glass. **Remember**, put the beater into the solution before turning on the beater. Leave the beater in the solution until the beater has stopped turning before you remove it from the mixture. If you remove the beater from the solution while it is still spinning you will have a 360 degree milk shake mess.

Pies

Coffee Spanish Creme Pie

If you really want to impress your child and/or your significant other, a pie is a good way to do it. For those of you who are of a certain age range you may remember that there is a book called "Real Men Don't Eat Quiche". Well, it probably should have been "Real Men Don't Make Pies". However, for our touchy, feely society and the new adaptability of the male creature, it is probably good that we can make a pie. Now, I am not big on knitting, crocheting, or cross-stitching, but a pie isn't really that bad.

Watch this, put a zap of coffee in it so you get a little high from the caffeine. In any case, here we go.

Ingredients:

1	Baked pie shell - 9 in.
3	Eggs
1 tps	Instant coffee
1 pkg.	Knox® Gelatin
3 cups	Milk
1/2 tps	Salt
2/3 cup	Sugar
1 tsp.	Vanilla extract

Tools:

Bowls, 2
Double Boiler (optional)
Measuring cup
Oven
Pan, Farber Wear
Pie Plate - 9 in.
Tablespoon
Teaspoon
Whisk

Take three cups of milk and put them into the sauce pan. You can use 2% milk to cut down on the fat or be decadent and use whole milk.

If the child wants to pour the milk into the measuring cup just make sure the child is strong enough to hold the milk container. A full gallon of milk can be too heavy for some four or five year olds.

If you have a one cup measuring cup the child can pour the milk into the saucepan. However, make sure the milk does not splash out. No matter how big the target, a child can miss when pouring liquid.

Put two teaspoons of instant coffee into the milk. You can use decaffeinated or regular coffee, depending on your preference.

Put the pack of gelatin into the pan of milk and let stand for five minutes.

Now put the saucepan on a stove unit and heat on medium heat or one half turn of the heat control.

You or the child needs to stir the milk with the tablespoon so that it does not stick to the bottom of the pan. The stirring also helps to dissolve the gelatin.

Now add 2/3 cup of sugar.

Now get the two bowls. One bowl is for the white part of the egg, the albumen, the other bowl is for the yellow part, the yolk.

You need to be careful on this step and make sure no pieces of egg shell go into the bowls.

Crack the egg a little. You need to crack it enough to get your thumbs into the crack. Separate the egg shell enough so that the white goes into one of the bowls.

When most of the white is out, you can open the shell wide and put the yolk into the other bowl.

Repeat this operation for the other two eggs.

If the child wants to help have them crack the egg while you hold it in the palm of your hand.

Now you need to beat the egg yolks with the whisk.

Slowly pour the heated milk into the egg yolk. Stir the mixture with the tablespoon as the milk is being poured in.

After everything has been mixed in the bowl, pour the contents of the bowl back into the saucepan.

> **Note:** My Mother, T. J.'s grandmother, has been making this dessert all her life. Don't pour the egg yolks into the saucepan. That would be wrong. This is somewhat like the situation where you are stirring the contents of a pot in a clockwise direction. Then you ask your child to stir it. The child stirs in the counter-clockwise direction and UN-stirs the contents.

When all the contents are in the saucepan, return the pan to the stove on medium heat. Stir constantly until the contents thicken. You know when it thickens because the concoction will coat the spoon.

Take the saucepan off the stove.

Add 1/2 teaspoon of salt and one teaspoon of vanilla extract. Stir until salt and vanilla mixes with the contents.

Now put the sauce pan in the refrigerator and allow to cool for two or three hours.

When the contents of the pan thicken, take it from the refrigerator.

Take the bowl with the egg whites and use the whisk to beat them. The egg whites will stiffen and coat the whisk.

Now fold (which is a cooking word for gently stir) the stiffened egg whites into the contents of the pan as the two are poured together.

Now, with everything in the saucepan, pour the contents into the baked pie shell.

Put back into the refrigerator to cool some more.

Serve with whipped cream, Dream Whip® or Redi Whip®.

Section 5 - Snacks

Fruit Treats

Let's face it, lots of times it is not the end product that is important, it is the effort and interest we give our children. With that thought in mind, I present a simple list of fruit snacks.

Grapefruit Half

Ingredients:

    Confectionery sugar (white, powdered sugar)
    Grapefruit
    Maraschino Cherries

Tools:

    Fruit knife

Put the top of the grapefruit, where it was attached to the tree, so that you are looking directly down on the grapefruit. Put your right index finger on this spot. Now rotate the grapefruit 90 degrees, or one-quarter a roll to the right with your finger.

Now cut the grapefruit in half.

What you now see are the little triangular parts of the grapefruit sections. If you cut the grapefruit through the place where it was connected to the tree, you would be making a mistake for this recipe.

Take the fruit knife and cut each individual triangular section. Do this without cutting the membrane separating each triangular section. Cut each triangular section deep enough so that it can be easily taken out with a fork or spoon.

After the cutting is finished, take a spoon and put a thin layer of confectionery sugar in a circle on the top.

Most children do not like the tart taste of grapefruit. The confectionery sugar reduces that tartness. The whiteness makes an interesting change from the regular granulated sugar.

Put a Maraschino cherry in the center or take out sections of the grapefruit and replace with a cherries. The cherries add color and sweetness.

Grapefruit in "Blood"

Ingredients:

    Grapefruit

Tool:

    Fruit Knife

Sometimes food can be made more interesting by association.

One does not normally think about "eating blood."

As you may have guessed, I am not talking about real blood, only something that looks like blood.

This recipe is good for breakfast. It gets the child's eyes open real fast when served.

Take a grapefruit and cut it in half across the sections, so that you can cut out the little triangular shaped fruit.

Put all the triangles into a bowl. Squeeze the grapefruit rind to get the juice into the dish.

Now add some Maraschino cherry juice. Use three teaspoons full of juice. If that is not red enough for you, add more to obtain the appropriate color.

Bananas and Dates

Ingredients:

    Banana(s)
    Dates, pitted

Tool:

    Fruit Knife

Bananas have potassium (chemical symbol "K"). Dates also have vitamins (I just do not know what they are).

You should have one banana per child.

Peel the banana(s).

Cut the banana(s) into slices. Point one end of the peeled banana towards your right hand and the other end toward your left hand. Now cut the banana in slices about one-quarter inch thick.

Take dates and cut them in half.

Place the banana slices on a plate. If you use a luncheon or dinner plate the surface of the plate is big enough for you to make a face. Use three slices for each eye. Use two slices for the nose. Use the remaining pieces for a smiley mouth - teeth with cavities. How festive?

Now put the halves of dates on the banana slices.

The child can use his/her fingers or a fork to eat.

Peanut Butter and Jelly Bagel Pizza

Ingredients:

Bagel, raisin cinnamon, preferable
Peanut Butter
Jelly

Tools:

Table knife
Teaspoon

Children like sweetness. Therefore, I suggest raisin cinnamon bagels.

You will need one bagel per child.

Cut the bagel into half so that you have two round halves.

Place on a plate with the flat side up. Put a layer of peanut butter on the bagel halves. Take a knife and cut into four sections, each.

Put the plate in the microwave. Push, CLEAR, TIME , 15 (for 15 seconds), and START.

This amount of time makes the bagel softer and melts a little of the peanut butter.

Take the teaspoon and a jelly your child likes. Put a little dab of jelly on each piece.

This is to be eaten like tiny pizza sections. As with the real pizza, serve with plenty of napkins or paper toweling sheets.

Math Munchies

This is a recipe that will require your child to use math — or starve.

Ingredients:

    1 box   Stoned Wheat Thins® (no, they are not on controlled substances). Get a box.
    8-12 slices Kraft®, sliced cheese.

Tools:

    None - believe it or not

I found that if I use Stoned Wheat Thins®, Wheat Crackers from Red Oval Farms and Kraft® Sliced Cheese, my son is motivated to do math in his head.

Here's the deal.

Stoned Wheat Thins® can be broken into two equal pieces along an indentation in the cracker.

Kraft® cheese slices can be broken into four equal pieces by folding them.

The following problems can be asked.

How many crackers do you need for one slice of cheese, if you can get the plastic wrap off the cheese?

If you want twelve (12) cracker and cheese treats, how many crackers and how many slices of cheese are needed?

If you only have three pieces of cheese, how many whole crackers do you need if you feed two to the dog?

If you plan on eating four whole crackers, how many slices of cheese do you need?

Get the idea?

If you wanted to be a real stinker, you can add a geography and spelling lesson to this project. You can ask the child to find where Red Oval Farms is located. You can then ask them to spell the place. (ANSWER: Look at the end of the box ... and I'm not kidding, is Etobicoke, Canada. The place sounds more like some life threatening disease than a place that would produce anything edible.)

Tangy Fruit Drink

Ingredients:

- 20 Black cherries
- 1 Cantaloupe
- 2 Grapefruit
- 2 Oranges
- 2 Peaches
- 20 Strawberries

Tools:

- Bowl
- Cutting/chopping board (or plastic)
- Knives

This is T. J.'s recipe, so I'll let him explain its preparation and consumption:

"You can add anything. You can add apples. You can add plums.

Slice the fruit in half. You cut it in the middle Take the seeds and the pits out.

You put the fruit into the blender or a juice maker. I like to squeeze the juice by hand.

You can also add other fruit, but what makes it so tangy is the lemon. You can also add lime, but mainly the lemon makes it very tangy!

You can serve this in a glass that has been in the freezer for a hour. The glass will be frosted. You can put little umbrellas in to make it fancy and it is great for parties or just to have a tangy fruit drink for any occasion."

Celery and Peanut Butter

Celery is a great source of dietary fiber. Peanut butter is a great source of energy. Combine these two together and you have something that is good for the child and something the child might eat.

Ingredients:

    Celery
    Peanut butter, chunky or smooth

Tools:

    Knife, sharp
    Table knife

Celery is an interesting vegetable, in my opinion. It grows in a "bunch" from the inside out in a very tight mass. The inside center is called the "heart", like a tree, and the outside is called "stalks". You buy celery by the "bunch."

I suggest you give the child, especially young child, the inner stalks near the heart. These are easiest to chew. The outer stalk can be hard and stringy; this is especially true of old bunches.

You need to pull each stalk off the bunch and wash each stalk under running water.

Celery is grown in rich (dark/black) dirt. While the outside stalks may look clean in the produce section of the grocery store to entice you to purchase it, you will find a lot of dirt on the stalks.

After you have the customary celery stalk fencing dual, you should cut the stalks in pieces about six inches long.

Now the child can fill the groove with peanut butter.

I suggest putting a little salt on them. This adds taste to both the peanut butter and the celery. You can also put strips of cheese on top. Just push the strips down into the peanut butter to hold them on.

Meat Roll-Ups

These are one of those treats that are easy for a Dad or children to do alone or together. It is a good source of protein (and fat) and it also gives the children some discretion in the decision making process.

Ingredients:

    Meat, sliced ham, roast beef, turkey, balogna, salami
    Cheese, sliced American, Swiss, White

Tools:

    Knife, table

Take a piece of meat. The meat can be a random slice from a deli or from one of those packs of round things that comes in plastic. Put a piece of cheese on the meat and roll it up.

As simple as that.

If you want to, you can use a tooth pick to hold roll up together. But, from my experience they are usually consumed as fast as they are rolled.

If you roll them, stick a tooth pick in them, and put them in the microwave on a plate for 20 seconds, the heat will melt the cheese a little and holds the meat and cheese together. When you take them out of the microwave, you can pull out the tooth pick(s) and throw them away. Hot roll ups are good on cold days and can make an interesting lunch.

The various combinations of meat and cheese can teach the child about counting theory.

Suppose you have five (5) meats: turkey, ham, salami, roast beef and bologna and you have three (3) cheeses: American, Swiss and white cheese.

What we are going to do is put one meat and one cheese together.

How many different combinations can be made?

Well, when it comes to T. J., he just experimented and did one of each, counted them, and ate them.

You can use a "logic tree" to solve the problem mathematically. Draw five lines from a point. These five branches represent the five meats. At the end of each branch draw three lines. These lines represent the three cheeses. Now count the end of each line. There are 15. This is 5 x 3: the number of meats times the number of cheeses.

You can put the cheese first and then the meats and the answer will still be the same.

Well, T. J. thought the math was interesting.

**Publications
You should know about**

"25 Common Cooking Mistakes ... and How to Avoid Them", *Cook's Illustrated,* 17 Station St. Brookline Village, MA 02147. Free!

Caring Families, Sue Nicholson Butkus, Ph.D., extension nutrition specialist, Cooperative Extension, Washington State University, Box 645912, Pullman, WA 99164-5912. $15.00.

Chef's Catalog ("Professional Restaurant Equipment for the Home Chef Since 1979"), 3215 Commercial Avenue, Northbrook, IL 60062-1900. Order toll-free, 24 hours a day at (800) 338-3232.

Cooking (Merit Badge pamphlet), Boy Scouts of America, Irving, Texas, 1995.

Edmund Scientific Company, 101 East Gloucester Pike, Barrington, NJ 08007-1380.
    Phone: (609) 547-8880
    FAX: (609) 573-6295
    Customer Service: (609) 573-6260

Environmental Nutrition, 52 Riverside Drive, New York, NY 10024. $424/yr.

The Growth of the Mind and the Endangered Origins of Intelligence, Stanley I. Greenspan, MD, (Addison-Wesley).

The Harvard Common Press, Publishers of Gambit Books, 535 Albany Street, Boston, MA 02118. Phone: (617)423-5803, FAX (617) 695-9794.

Marnie's Kitchen Shortcuts, Marnie Swedberg (St. Martin's Griffin). $11.95.

Morton Salt "Household Hints"
    Morton International, Inc.
    Morton Salt
    Chicago, IL   60606-1597

Quaker Oats Company
    www.quakeroatmeal.com

Roughing It Easy, Dian Thomas, (Warner Books Edition), 1975.

Secrets of Fat-Free Cooking, Sandra Woodruff, RD, nutrition consultant (Avery Publishing Group). $13.95.

Scout Field Book, Boy Scouts of America.

Triathlon, a Triple Fitness Sport, Sally Edwards (endorsed by the United States Triathlon Association), Contemporary Books, Inc. (Chicago)1983, 296 pages.

Triathloning For Ordinary Mortals, Steven Jonas, M.D., W.W. Norton & Company (New York) 1986, 288 pages.

Turkey All Year, Susan O. Byrne, (Barcaly-Ramsey Associates, P.O. Box 7122, Arlington, VA 22207), 1984

**<u>Organizations
You should know about</u>**

American Academy of Pediatrics
    Division of Publications
    141 Northwest Point Blvd.
    P.O. Box 927
    Elk Grove Village, IL 60009-0927
        "Feeding Kids Right Isn't Always Easy"
        "Parent Resource Guide"

American Institute for Cancer Research
    1759 R. Street, NW
    Washington, DC 20069
    Phone: (202) 328-7744
        "The AICR Health & Nutrition Resource Catalog"

Center for Science in the Public Interest
    1875 Connecticut Avenue, N.W.
    Suite 300
    Washington, DC 20009-5728
    Phone: (202) 332-9110
        Publishes the *Nutrition Action Healthletter* ($19.95/yr.).

Food & Drug Administration, Adverse Reaction Monitoring System
    Phone: (301) 443-1240
        Studies adverse reactions to additives

International Food Information Council Foundation
    Box 65708
    Washington, DC 20035.
       "Asthma & Food"

National Sleep Foundation
    Fourth Floor
    729 Fifteenth Street, N.W.
    Washington, DC 20005
    Phone: (202) 347-3471
    FAX: (202) 347-3472
    E-mail: natsleep@erols.com

Public Voice for Food & Health Policy
    1101 14th Street, N.W.
    Suite 700
    Washington, DC 20005
    Phone: (202) 371-1840

Cooking Measurements

dash	=	6 or 7 drops
pinch	=	less than 1/8 teaspoon
1/4 teaspoon	=	15 drops
1 teaspoon	=	1/3 tablespoon
1 tablespoon	=	3 teaspoons
2 tablespoons	=	1 fluid ounce (oz.)
4 tablespoons	=	1/4 cup or 2 fluid ozs.
8 tablespoons	=	1/2 cup or 4 fluid ozs.
16 teaspoons	=	1 cup
1 cup	=	8 fluid ozs. or 1/2 pint
2 cups	=	1 pint
1/2 pint	=	small child
1 pint	=	16 fluid ounces
4 cups	=	1 quart
1 quart	=	32 fluid ounces
4 quarts	=	1 gallon (U.S.)

Glossary of Cooking Terms

Bake — To cook by dry heat as in conventional oven or in aluminum foil. Recipes that do not work are called "half-baked."

Baste — To moisten food with a liquid while cooking such as using melted fat, drippings, or special sauces. You baste a turkey or put barbecue sauce on chicken.

Boil — To cook in water or other liquid hot enough to bubble (100° Celsius, 212° Fahrenheit, or 373° Kelvin).

Braise — To cook meat tender by browning in hot fat, then cooking in covered pan, usually with added liquid.

Broil — To cook meat directly over or in front of an open fire.

Deep Fry — To cook by immersion in very hot fat or oil.

Dredge — To coat meat with flour, often seasoned, before browning or frying.

Fry — To cook in an open pan with small amount of fat or oil.

Marinate	To tenderize or flavor meat by covering with spiced vinegar or oil, salad dressing, or commercial marinade sauce.
Pan Broil	To cook meat in a very hot skillet with a minimum of fat. This method makes it possible to cook food by broiling over a gas or electric stove.
Poach	To cook just below the boiling point of water.
Roast	To cook meat and vegetables in hot air, as in a covered pan in an oven or in aluminum foil covered by coals.
Sauté	To cook meat by searing, then simmering until tender, usually with vegetables added. Also, to cook vegetables and fruit (often dry fruit).
Scald	To heat to just below the boiling point.
Sear	To seal surfaces of meat by exposing to intense heat so that juices are contained.
Simmer	To cook in liquid just barely at the boiling point.
Tenderize	To render meat easier to cook or chew by softening the tissues by pounding, with chemicals, or by marinating.

NOTES

NOTES

NOTES

YOUR RECIPE

YOUR RECIPE